PRACTICALLY SPEAKING:
An Illustrated Guide

•

The game, guns and gear of the
International Defensive Pistol Association
with real-world applications

By Walt Rauch

RAUCH & COMPANY, LTD.
Lafayette Hill, PA 19444

Copyright© 2002 by R. Walter Rauch

All rights reserved. Except for use in a review, no portion of this book may be reproduced in any form without the express written permission of the publisher.

Neither the author nor the publisher assumes any liability for any damage or injury of any kind that may result from the use or misuse of the information contained in this book.

Library of Congress Control Number: 2002091249

ISBN 0-9663260-1-6

Layout and Design by Detrich Design

Published by:
RAUCH & COMPANY, LTD.
Lafayette Hill, PA 19444

Printed in the United States of America

To Kathie,
my wife:
Although life ends,
love is eternal.

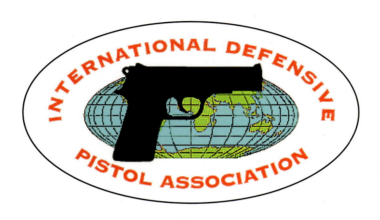

WEBSITE: WWW.IDPA.COM

ACKNOWLEDGEMENTS

Many have contributed to this handbook. The International Defensive Pistol Association owes its existence to Bill Wilson, who gathered together Ken Hackathorn, John Sayle, Dick Thomas, Larry Vickers and me for the Founding Conference in Marietta, Ohio in October, 1996. Without Bill Wilson, there would be no IDPA. Without the collective experience of the founding members, we would not have the solid rules on which IDPA is built.

My thanks to all those who enthusiastically supported the fledgling organization and gave so much of their time, money and expertise to getting IDPA off the ground. Larry Bullock deserves special recognition for his unflagging efforts. Early sponsors who had faith in the IDPA concept include Smith & Wesson and Springfield Armory. Bill Wilson and his company, Wilson Combat, Inc., have continued to give the mother's milk of any new organization – time and money.

Thanks also to PrimeMedia *Handguns* and Harris Publications' *Combat Handguns* magazines for permission to use both text and photos originally published in those venues.

For the photography work, I thank Rob Adam, Frank James, John Lysak, Joe Venezia, Kerby Smith, Chris Edwards, the late Roger Tucker, Bob Thomsen and more than a few shooters whose names escape me who kindly took photos while I shot a course of fire.

For final manuscript content, I asked for and got advice from Michael Bane, Denise Jackson, Chris Edwards, Frank James and Jim Glendening. For the editorial work – putting the words together in logical and readable form – my wife Kathie once again has succeeded in making me look good.

The author shoots the classic S&W Model 10, a .38 Special 4"-barrel blue steel revolver.

TABLE OF CONTENTS

PREFACE		9
CHAPTER ONE:	What Is IDPA?	11
CHAPTER TWO:	The "Game" and Self-Defense	15
CHAPTER THREE:	Get the Right Gear	19
CHAPTER FOUR:	Shoot in All Divisions	25
CHAPTER FIVE:	Concealed-Carry Draw	30
CHAPTER SIX:	Strong- and Weak-Hand Shooting	32
CHAPTER SEVEN:	One-Hand and Retention Shooting	34
CHAPTER EIGHT:	Engaging Targets - In Priority and/or Sequence	36
CHAPTER NINE:	Shooting on the Move	38
CHAPTER TEN:	Using Cover and "Slicing the Pie"	40
CHAPTER ELEVEN:	Low Cover/Kneeling	42
CHAPTER TWELVE:	Seated Shooting Positions	44
CHAPTER THIRTEEN:	Going Prone	46
CHAPTER FOURTEEN:	Practical Reloads	48
CHAPTER FIFTEEN:	Dim-Light Shooting	50
CHAPTER SIXTEEN:	Designing IDPA Courses of Fire	53
CHAPTER SEVENTEEN:	IDPA Classifier CL-0001	71
CHAPTER EIGHTEEN:	Scoring System	77
CONCLUSION		78

PREFACE

"The Use of Defensive Arms In a Sporting Environment" is how I see the purpose of the International Defensive Pistol Association (IDPA). The reasons for competing in this sport vary with the participant. Some take part to sharpen gun handling skills and/or to learn, apply or review the skills and tactics that accompany using a firearm in self-defense. Others just flat out enjoy winning at anything in which they participate.

In all this, no one should confuse "Sport" with "Training." One doesn't normally play a baseball game and score the results while at the same time expect to learn how to play the game. Skills development is properly reserved for practice, with a coach. So, too, should self-defense skills be learned.

If this premise is understood, the critics who posit that by taking part in gun games, you develop habits, practices and techniques that are detrimental to real-world survival skills are wrong. I base my own opinion on observing and knowing a large number of very capable gunmen who have enjoyed – and continue to play – the games and yet are quite able to distinguish the difference in application. They, and I, never have any problem understanding that paper and steel targets don't shoot back.

IDPA, IPSC and other dynamic firearms sports give back to you those things that you are seeking: ability, personal development, or ego fulfillment through peer recognition. You decide what you want and play the game accordingly. Since IDPA is the new game in town so to speak, to understand the why and the how of IDPA's formation and the interest in it by over 9,000 members, we need to look at the granddaddy of all modern dynamic practical pistol competitions, the International Practical Shooting Confederation (IPSC), founded in 1975 by Jeff Cooper and a group of like-minded students during a handgun training class conducted by Mr. Cooper at Ray Chapman's (now Green Valley) Range in Columbia, Missouri.

"The Founding Conference" established eight principles to define practical shooting competitions. I've taken the liberty of extracting what I consider to be the essence of the rules from the complete text as found in the November 1994 edition of the IPSC Rule Book, as follows:

1 - Practical competition is open to all reputable persons...
2 - Accuracy, power and speed are the equivalent elements...
3 - ...firearm types are not separated, all compete together without handicap...
4 - ...a test of expertise in the uses of practical firearms and equipment...
5 - ...is conducted using practical targets...
6 - The challenge presented in practical competition must be realistic...
7 - Practical competition is diverse. Within the limits of realism, problems are constantly changed, never permitting unrealistic specialization of either technique or equipment...
8 - Practical competition is free style...the problem is posed in general and the participant is permitted the freedom to solve it...

IPSC was envisioned by the founders to be a format in which competition was to be done with "practical guns and gear." Observing current IPSC events, it is obvious that some of the principles have been upheld while others have been abandoned. IPSC and its USA representative organization, the United States Practical Shooting Association (USPSA), continue to offer a very dynamic and challenging sport, but that sport has shifted, at the behest of the membership, to much more of a flat-out shooting contest that now requires guns particularly crafted to meet the demands of the competition. This would be all well and good if the courses of fire hewed to the realistic use of a handgun, but being required to fire twenty or more rounds in one stage does not remotely approximate real-world encounters by the legally-armed non-sworn citizen.

The governing bodies of the organizations are making changes to more accurately reflect the founding principles (and, in truth, in response to the phenomenal growth of IDPA), but this may well be a case of too little, too late. My observation is that both IDPA's formation and growing ranks are partially due to the maturing of IPSC, its attempt to be all things to all people, and years of interpretations and re-interpretations applied to the simple principles as put down by Mr. Cooper, which dilute and continue to compromise and negate the founding principles. Not good or bad, but this is IPSC as it exists today. This leads us to the Principles of IDPA.

But first, we need to establish the ground rules of safe gun handling, which I've compiled into the following list:

Rauch's Rules
of Safe Gun Handling

1. *All guns are always loaded!*

2. Don't put your finger on the trigger until you are ready to fire.

3. Don't point the gun at anything you are not willing to destroy.

4. Always be sure that your target and the surrounding area is safe; that is, *no one is present in any possible bullet impact area.*

5. When picking up a firearm, the first thing you do is open the gun's action to insure that it is unloaded, no matter who had it last or that you just put it down. Also, it is not safe to either accept a gun from, or give a gun to, another person without first insuring that the gun is safe. This is best done by opening the action and keeping it this way while passing the gun *with the muzzle pointed in a safe direction* – i.e., not pointed at you, the recipient or anyone else.

6. *Everyone* on a firing range must wear eye and ear protection. This includes spectators. The ricochet or defective gun does not discriminate between shooter and bystander.

7. Use quality ammunition. Don't shoot junk! Don't shoot "the other guy's" reloads. He may have a very devil-may-care attitude toward his well being. Yes, good ammo costs more, but what are your body parts worth to you?

8. Booze, drugs and guns really don't mix! A drunk or over-medicated person with a gun is more dangerous than a pyromaniac with a match. If this isn't clear to you...get rid of your guns!

9. Keep guns out of the hands of children and others when you are not present by storing them properly and safely.

10. Read – and follow – the firearm's manufacturer's instruction manual.

CHAPTER ONE
What is IDPA?

What is the International Defensive Pistol Association (IDPA)? It's "The *real* Practical Shooting sport." IDPA was formed by Bill Wilson, John Sayle, Dick Thomas, Ken Hackathorn, Larry Vickers and me at a meeting held in Marietta, Ohio in October, 1996. In essence, IDPA has been created to redirect the conduct of sporting competitions that use defensive handguns.

The founders, all veterans of decades of practical shooting, saw there was a need to re-examine, redirect and revitalize practical defensive shooting. We saw that the guns and the courses of fire, as well as the overemphasis on big prizes has, bluntly put, misdirected practical shooting from its first and founding principle – the learning and practice of defensive shooting in a sporting environment. IDPA is based on the concept that the shooter, not the equipment nor the caliber used, is the most important factor in the defensive equation.

We founders drew on our experience in other shooting sports, real-world applications and the teaching of weapon craft to establish the principles and the rules necessary for a self-defense-based handgun sport. We recognized that IDPA would not and could not be the end-all of tactical firearms contests. We developed a mission statement which is, quoting from the IDPA Official Rule Book, "The IDPA goal is quite simply the use of practical equipment, including full-charge service ammunition, to solve simulated 'real-world' self-defense scenarios. Shooters competing in Defensive Pistol events are required to use practical handguns and holsters that are truly suitable for self-defense use. No 'competition-only' equipment is permitted.....since the main goal is to test the skill and ability of the individual, not their equipment or gamesmanship."

IDPA is also a trophy-only sport and no cash or merchandise awards are made. Trophies or plaques can be awarded to the top shooters in each division and class. Product prizes may be awarded, but only by "chance" drawings. And all divisions are totally separate from each other.

Within each division, the classifications are: Marksman, Sharpshooter, Expert and Master. These are determined by shooting a standard classifier and then, based on established values set by IDPA, the local club official certifies the shooter's rating. The intent of the entire system is that a club can fulfill all its needs at the club level, without the necessity of a national headquarters and its bureaucracy.

The principles and the divisions of competition, again quoting from the rule book, are:
- To create a level playing field for all competitors to test the skill and ability of the individual, not their equipment or gamesmanship.
- To promote safe and proficient use of guns and equipment suitable for self-defense use.
- To offer a competition forum for shooters using standard, factory-produced service pistols such as the Beretta 92F, Glock 17, etc. in **Stock Service Pistol (SSP) Division**; for shooters using popular single-action 9x19mm/.40S&W pistols which have been modified for carry in **Enhanced Service Pistol (ESP) Division**; 1911-style single-stack .45ACPs which have been modified for carry, not competition, fall in **Custom Defensive Pistol (CDP) Division**; and service revolvers such as the Smith & Wesson Model 686 caliber .38 Special/.357 magnum are in **Stock Service Revolver (SSR) Division**. There is a fifth division, **Back-Up Gun (BUG)**, that is authorized for use only at club-level events. (See Chapter 4.)
- To provide shooters with practical and realistic courses of fire that simulate a potentially life-threatening encounter or test skills required in such an eventuality.

The leadership of IDPA is also to be responsive to both shooters and sponsors by maintaining a firm stability of rules.

The ammunition power factor (PF) is 125,000 for all but .45ACP, which is 165,000. An exception is made in SSR Division, where all use the 125,000 PF. (To calculate PF, take the bullet weight and multiply it by its velocity as determined by firing the round over a chronograph. The result must meet or exceed the listed PF.)

Revolvers may only be loaded with six rounds and have a maximum barrel length of 4". (Larger-capacity revolvers may be used, but may only be loaded with six rounds.) Semi-autos in calibers less than .45ACP can have a maximum of 10 rounds loaded in the magazine, plus one in the chamber (the official condition of readiness to begin any stage). The 1911 .45ACP division (CDP) restricts mag capacity to eight rounds and one in the chamber. (But if you use a seven-round mag anywhere, then all your mags can only have seven rounds in them. You cannot pick and choose magazine capacity to gain a competitive advantage; in other words, no gaming!)

All holsters and magazine carriers are required to be *practical* rigs worn at or behind the hip, with the exception that for revolvers, two speed loaders may be worn forward of the strong-side holster. IDPA defines what is "practical" by specifying the holsters that are allowed in its rule book Appendix. *If it's not listed, it's not allowed.* (Exceptions will be made for non-US rigs and for new gear as it comes to market.) If it's a speed rig designed to give a perceived "edge," it's not allowed. The Board of Directors recognized the vast number of holster manufacturers worldwide and to facilitate the introduction of the sport, confined the holster review to those found in the United States.

One of the bulwarks of IDPA is course design – *realistic* course design. Each stage should make sense. The shooter should be able to look at and understand the problem presented as having some relevancy to defensive use of a handgun…a course of fire that, when viewed, you say to yourself, "Yes, this could happen – and quite possibly could or did happen to me." Now I'm not saying that every stage in every match will be realistic (no one is perfect, to be sure), but the match directors and course designers are trying their best. IDPA furnishes a Course of Fire book for them to choose from and modify as necessitated by local constrictions.

IDPA also provides some pretty firm rules and guidelines on how to design and set up stages, including a limit on the number of "no-shoot" targets (you can have one no-shoot for every three shoot targets), maximum distance between shooting positions (10 yards), no shooting boxes and a limit on the number of rounds that can be fired in any one stage (18 rounds). In addition, scenario-based targets should be no further away from the shooter than 15 yards, with *occasional* exceptions. No, you won't find perfection, but you'll find good faith effort to be sure.

Is IDPA for you? Well, the best way to find out is to visit a local match, but don't shoot; just watch and ask questions. You'll find that all you need is a gun, three mags or speed loaders, the above-mentioned holster and about 100 rounds of ammo. "Seeing is believing" is an oft-quoted and true statement. (More about guns and gear in Chapter Three.)

As an example, at one typical local club match held at the Easton Fish & Game Association in Easton, PA, the match director, Ted Murphy, expected a light turnout because he had neglected to send out the previous month's match results with the usual exhortation to come out and shoot. Well, without prompting, 50 shooters showed for the four-stage match. As I pulled up I noted there was the obligatory safety area set aside for gun handling, putting on gear and generally checking equipment. After a short safety briefing and an overview of all the stages, the shooters broke up into squads.

I was struck by the diversity of guns and gear being used. It's safe to say that the Kydex/polymer holster (and mag pouches) are now the equivalent of the ubiquitous nylon belt slide for IDPA work. There were a few of the belt slides there, too. The dominant gun was a toss up between the Glock and the 1911. I would have guessed the Glock 17 in 9mm to be the favored gun/caliber choice, but this is not the case. The Glock models and calibers included the Model 36 in .45ACP, a Model 32 in .357 SIG (with full loads), a Model 19 and a few Model 17s in 9mm. The Ruger semi-auto in 9mm and .40 S&W made an appearance, as did the S&W Model 625 in .45ACP and the Model 38 five-shot .38 Special 2"-barrel revolver. (Yes, one determined – and proficient – gentleman shot the entire match with his 2" gun and did fairly well.) But the one competitor who really rated a second look was the guy with the Russian-designed Tokarev worn in, what else, a belt slide holster.

I go to a lot of matches and have for over 30 years. I've only seen Tokarevs used in matches run by my friend Ken Hackathorn, who likes to do "pick-up gun" events, where the competitor has to pick up a gun down range and use it to finish the stage. Ken has used a Tokarev more than once, but I've never, ever seen anyone who voluntarily chose to use this gun in a practical shooting event. For the limited amount of time that I observed the shooter and the gun, he was not at all disadvantaged. One reason might be that recently-imported Tokarevs have an external add-on manual safety. It doesn't work smoothly, but it's better than relying on the original design that has only a half-cock "safety notch" for carry. Also, this gun had a 9mm barrel installed, so it was a legal caliber for IDPA.

The competitor mix was just as eclectic as the guns. Ages ran from the young'uns to some who have cashed a fair share of Social Security checks. Some were very content to get through the match with their carry gun, while others were trying to win their class. And in a parody of the correct phrase, they did all "just get along." Seeing *is* believing.

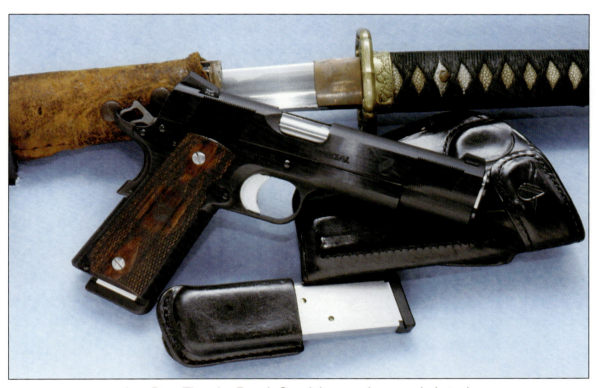

Les Baer Thunder Ranch Special...a modern warrior's tool.

CHAPTER TWO ~ The "Game" and Self-defense

The author uses two guns to solve a "real-world" scenario problem.

The author follows the IDPA rule of "at least one knee on the ground" while using low cover. The "game" has some real-life application.

CHAPTER TWO
The "Game" and Self-defense

Will playing the game help or hurt self-defense ability? Actually, the larger question to ask is, "Does playing any defensive handgun game help or hurt your 'survivability' in a real-world encounter?" Well, as the politicians would say, "it depends." How you approach the matter and what your expectations are determine the results. If you think all you have to do to get top-shelf self-defense training is join IDPA or IPSC, pay a minimal match fee and shoot a local contest, you are going to be very disappointed and, as usually follows, your unhappiness will screw up everyone else's day at the match.

IDPA is a game; IPSC is a game. Most every shooting sport that fairly and objectively scores the contestants will not, and *cannot*, replicate or even come close to real-life encounters. The scenarios do attempt to simulate some of the problems you might well encounter in everyday life, but IDPA will *not* provide the training you should have and can get at academies like Thunder Ranch and Gunsite, to name but two such entities.

First off, as it has often been wryly observed, there are no rules in a gunfight. Clint Smith, director of Thunder Ranch, Inc., coined the phrase, "Always cheat! Always win!" OK, you can take the cynical approach and point out that this advice is certainly followed by some in the shooting sports, but this is just being a smart ass. All sports have rules so that everyone gets a level playing field and all participants can enjoy the contest with reasonable expectations that if they perform well they will be recognized by trophies or cash awards. In IDPA, the founders identified certain commonalities in using a firearm for self-defense and incorporated these into the rules. By following IDPA rules, newcomers are exposed to the basics of self-defense and through repetition during the contests they assimilate a working knowledge of those basics.

For example, it may come as a surprise to those who are already deeply involved in defensive weapon training to realize that no one is born with the knowledge and ability to be able to recognize and use cover. Indeed, most folks, when confronted with a living, breathing threat, stand fixed in place, dumbfounded and flatfooted despite their realization that a ten-ton truck of bad news is about to run them down! IDPA contests provide a means to overcome this, for many IDPA rules *require* that self-defense skills such as using cover, tactical reloading and moving while engaging threats be performed.

You're expected to think about what you do as it would apply in real self-defense. (It is a contest, though, so running away isn't an option!) The use of cover is accentuated and you are to engage threats as you see them when leaning out from behind cover. You shoot threats based on their proximity to you, closest ones first. Magazines or cylinders have to be reloaded in IDPA, too, but more tactically than in other games – i.e., when the semi-auto gun locks open or, as it is termed, goes to slide-lock, or the revolver cylinder goes "click," "click," "click" (also known as "empty gun indicators"). And, unlike other games, you must save your partially-empty magazines to meet the IDPA requirement to bring your gun up to full capacity before leaving cover. In the real world, you don't have an unlimited supply of ammunition.

Practical, concealable holsters are the rule and many contests mandate that all shooting be done "from concealment." (A good gauge of concealment is that none of your defensive equipment is visible to a viewer when you stand with both arms extended straight out to your sides, although revolver users may have two ammo pouches visible if worn forward of the holster.)

The scenarios or stages of fire are the heart of using a handgun in defensive sporting competition. The problem presented has to be real and relevant. To tell a competitor that he is to neutralize fifteen targets while negotiating an obstacle course – well, this might be "real" for a military operation, but not for self-defense (and the chances of someone surviving this challenge armed only with a handgun are slim to none). But, put the shooter in an easy chair with a TV set down range and have two or three targets partially hidden by a door frame simulating a home invasion. Now you are coming closer to reality. Throw in a stage where you, the shooter, are at an ATM machine and are accosted by two threat targets behind you about three feet away and you are coming much closer to what might happen in real life.

Self-defense problems are solved, according to published statistics, with the mere presentation of a handgun eighty percent of the time and with fewer than six rounds fired when the gun is used. As previously stated, IDPA rules limit the stage round count to 18. Targets are, normally, not permitted to be more than 15 yards away, and any movement within the problem is limited to no more than 10 yards – testing shooting and moving within reason rather than creating a track meet.

By the way, one IDPA Course of Fire (COF) which is excellent for practicing some of the fundamentals of self-defense is the Defensive Pistol Classification Match, IDPA CL-0001. This COF includes many of the commonly-accepted tactical and firing techniques and is good to use to practice your IDPA game skills and to sharpen your defensive abilities, depending on how you approach the stage requirements, which include shooting from a high and low barricade, shooting on the move while retreating and advancing, standing to engage or turning to engage single and multiple targets and non-dominant-hand shooting. Tactical and slide-lock reloads are included. How you shoot it determines if you are more interested in survival or winning.

When using the barricade in this stage, the IDPA rule on the use of cover requires only that more than 50% of the shooter's torso, and his entire lower body, must be behind the barricade. (For a more in-depth explanation, see Chapter 10.) For self-defense, I suggest you only expose the minimum amount of you and your gun to do the job. Also, when moving from the barricade forward to low cover behind the barrel, IDPA only requires that you have one knee on the ground. If you think in terms of incoming rounds, you'd scrunch down a whole lot further than this.

As I noted, this COF has just about everything in it that you might need for self-defense and an IDPA match (other than luck!): turning, moving, cover, weak-hand-only, strong-hand-only and two-handed shooting at single and multiple targets. If your self-defense training has degenerated into simply punching holes in a silhouette target at seven yards until you're knee-deep in brass or you want to get up to speed before attending an IDPA match, this COF is a great place to start. (Since this is the primary IDPA classification COF, you can shoot this and compare your scores with the rankings for Marksman, Sharpshooter, Expert and Master for each of the Divisions.)

In IDPA, you can enjoy a handgun sport using your real-world self-defense handgun rather than a gun designed or gunsmithed solely to provide a competitive edge. And of course, in some instances, modifications for sport can work *against* the gun's use for self-defense.

Next, IDPA encourages, but does not mandate, the use of full-power self-defense ammunition, for factory ammo does vary greatly and most serious shooters reload. As previously noted, IDPA uses a common power factor for each division that allows similar guns to compete on a more or less equal footing. At the present time, the rules are overly generous, allowing the 9mm, .40 and .45 to go head-to-head in some of the divisions and, human nature being what it is, there are those – more interested in winning than skills development – who run the edge with the lightest ammo permitted. But nothing stops you (except your ego) from using factory-equivalent ammo to be better able to manage your defensive firearm.

Only holsters suitable for continuous daily wear and that are designed for concealment are permitted. To emphasize this, many IDPA stages are shot with the gun concealed under a jacket or vest. Here again, a dyed-in-the-wool competitor can push the rules and use a less-ideal concealment rig, but he only cheats himself. By the way, if there is one headache for the administrators of IDPA, it is the ongoing review of holsters that are allowed to be used, because what is a concealment rig for one person is an abomination on another's belt. The IDPA Board of Directors has faced this problem head on, as I mentioned earlier, and lists those rigs that are OK and those that are disallowed.

You can use and wear only two magazine loaders that must be, like the holsters, worn behind your hip. (Revolver users can wear two speed loaders just forward of the holster, with another one behind the holster.) You can *carry* as many mags, etc. as you want, but you can only *wear* what is listed, for in real life only an exceptional few would choose to festoon themselves with spare ammo. (Not a bad thing, mind you; just not normal.) Actually, with the combination of gun restrictions and the listing of concealment holsters, a participant in IDPA matches can easily determine exactly what will and won't work for his daily needs, and he has a chance to network with others to see what they have found that works.

CHAPTER TWO ~ The "Game" and Self-defense

If and when you decide to try your hand at IDPA shooting, I strongly suggest following my advice in Chapter 1 of visiting a local match just to watch and ask questions. This will save you money and the embarrassment of showing up to shoot with the wrong gear, although most match directors will allow a "newbie" to shoot anyway if this happens. Of course, if you're really anxious to get started, you may well be able to buy (at reasonable cost) or borrow some gear right there.

Also, most importantly – learn the rules! Even if you are a Grand Master in another handgun sport, each game has its own play book and it's only common courtesy to follow the other guy's rules in his game. Sure, the match director and other shooters will bend over backward to help, but why not make the whole thing easier on everyone. Now all you have to do is go to a match, keep your hits in the five zone – and do it with real guns and gear! (IDPA rules allow a non-member to shoot one match. After that, he is expected to join IDPA if he wants to continue to participate.)

Critics of IDPA courses of fire and IDPA rules devised and applied for the safe conduct of these courses point out, correctly, that if the course is viewed as a real-world life-threatening situation, the mandated rules are not tactically correct and then they decry IDPA as being impractical. IDPA rules and courses of fire are, not surprisingly, designed and applied to firearms ranges, not the street. "Down range" is the operative term and gun muzzles (and bullets) are expected to be fired in a generally forward direction, with some latitude allowing shots to be fired to the left or right of the shooter, depending on range construction. But no rounds are permitted to be fired directly "up range," a fact much-appreciated by fellow competitors, safety officers and spectators.

Yes, this *is* artificial, since the real world is a 360-degree environment. However, designing and administering a 360-degree course of fire is not for the timid or the novice – and accidents *still* happen (people get shot!), but are accepted as part of advanced training. One retired trainer from a European Special Forces group told me his regiment loses two or three recruits each year. He added that, "This is God's way of telling them they didn't belong in the regiment!"

For example, shooting guns from inside a car is OK (wearing *two sets* of ear protection – inserts and muffs – is a good idea). But then asking competitors to exit with gun in hand (trigger finger straight along side the frame and out of the trigger guard, please!) so that they can scurry to the rear or to the engine or axle sections to engage targets is not really a bright idea when you're the Safety Officer who must be near to the shooter to assist him if necessary, verify that gun handling safety is being observed and run a timer as well. So, yes, the critics are correct. IDPA rules and courses of fire, due to safety being of paramount importance, often do not permit the correct tactical solution to the real-life scenarios they mimic. After all, no one is shooting back!

John Lysak shoots the Glock Model 35 in .40 caliber, good for self-defense and competition.

To restate the obvious, IDPA is *not* tactical training. IDPA is simply, as we pointed out earlier, the use of practical equipment, including full-charge service ammunition, to solve simulated self-defense scenarios in a controlled, safe setting. For tactical training, go to a training academy. For defensive skills application in a competitive environment, go to an IDPA match!

CHAPTER THREE ~ Get the Right Gear

S&W N-frame 4"-barrel revolver; Safariland holster

S&W N-frame 5"-barrel revolver; Kydex rig

Glock Model 36; Del Fatti concealment rig

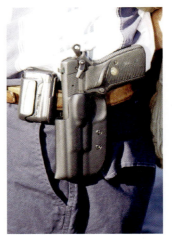

Browning High-Power; Kydex holster

S&W N-frame 3"-barrel revolver; custom leather

Para-Ordnance widebody 1911; Kydex holster

Taurus PT-92 with custom grips; Kydex holster

S&W double-action-only semi-auto; Kydex holster

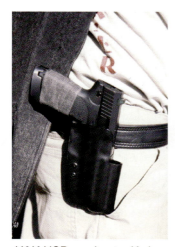

H&K USP semi-auto; Kydex holster

Venezia Custom 1911; concealment belt slide

S&W N-frame with custom grips; Kydex holster

Beretta Elite II; Safariland holster

CHAPTER THREE
Get the Right Gear

When you do decide to try your hand at IDPA shooting and go to a local match to watch and ask questions, that first question is usually, "Do I have the right gun and gear for the game?" Then, "What *should* I get." And, finally, you hear a little voice asking, "What do the winners use?" To answer these questions, aside from your own observations and comments from other shooters at the match, you can consult the IDPA rule book. Under **Equipment,** this guideline is offered: "All equipment used in Defensive Pistol matches must meet the following simple guidelines: equipment must be practical for self-defense use, concealable, suitable for all-day continuous wear and must be worn in a manner that would be appropriate for all-day continuous wear. ....if you wouldn't carry it to defend yourself, you can't shoot or use it in Defensive Pistol competition."

The founders do all carry guns for self-defense and have all competed in other "practical shooting" sports where the guns and equipment have become extremely specialized. The end result of this has been the spectacle of watching competitors carrying their scope-mounted, high-capacity, compensated guns to the line in a gun bag, then carefully mounting them in orthopedic devices for the purpose of shooting copious quantities of custom-loaded specialty ammo at target arrays that remind one of the Battle of the Little Big Horn, with thousands of hostiles pitted against a lone defender. Great fun, certainly, but not the *practical* use of a handgun!

We want IDPA to offer a competition forum for shooters to use standard or slightly-modified pistols in realistic scenarios. This means that the guns, holsters and ammo are of the type that would be normally carried and used for self-defense. The problem is that reality creeps into your choice. If you never have to use your carry gun, then the lightest and smallest is often chosen for comfort, convenience and ease of concealment. But, if you do have occasion to call on your personal defense arm, then you'll appreciate having brought the biggest gun, caliber and capacity available in a handgun to the fight. "A good big man will beat a good little man," the saying goes. Using a full-sized or slightly-compacted service arm in an IDPA contest will produce higher scores, just as it will for self-defense. You make the choice.

This having been said, contrary to most every other Action Shooting sport, the guns used in IDPA can be fiddled with, but only a little bit. You can change sights and grips, have internal action work done to improve function and accuracy and put on a custom finish. But you can't muck it up with heavy barrels or compensators, change to some trick sight or appreciably alter the gun's overall original configuration. Depending on the division, you may add extended thumb safeties, bevel mag wells and use a full-length guide rod, as long as it is not heavier than common steel. For more control on gun modifications, IDPA uses a specific-sized box in which the competitor's gun must fit (revolvers excluded). The box measures 8 3/4" x 6" x 1 5/8". The gun, including magazine, cannot weigh more than 43 ounces.

Magazine capacity restrictions are in place for a couple of reasons. First, IDPA's courses of fire are realistic and as such a perceived need for a 23-round mag doesn't exist in all but a fight against the Mongol hordes. Second, high-capacity mags are expensive and the normal defensive handgun owner should be

Ken Hackathorn (left), an IDPA co-founder, conducts an equipment inspection before an IDPA National Championship match.

CHAPTER THREE ~ Get the Right Gear

Ernest Langdon uses what little concealment he has while shooting this IDPA course of fire.

An aggressive stance controls recoil. Note the IWB (inside-the-waistband) rig for this big revolver.

Scott Gilbertson lowers his profile by going to one knee while protecting a "downed comrade" in this match scenario.

CHAPTER THREE ~ Get the Right Gear

able to afford to shoot without taking out a second mortgage on his home. While there are restrictions on capacity, you can use your high-capacity magazine guns (as long as they comply with the rules); you just don't load the mag to full capacity.

Regarding how to decide just what is a "practical" holster, what the Supreme Court judge said about pornography, "I can't define it, but I know it when I see it," somewhat also applies to holsters for IDPA. There is and never will be any unanimous agreement on this subject and to not have rules leaves the sport open to the introduction of those orthopedic devises I mentioned masquerading as holsters. As such, the IDPA Board of Directors makes the call and does provide a listing of approved rigs in the rule book Appendix, as pointed out earlier. If a holster isn't on

Allen Cooley crouches to maximize his use of cover... not required by IDPA rules, but very real.

the approved list, the owner or manufacturer should submit it to IDPA for approval. It's safe to figure that, as I noted in Chapter One, if it's a speed rig designed to give a perceived "edge," it's not allowed. If the holster is listed in the competition section of a catalog, save your money.

The "at or behind the hip" rule, again, is pretty straight forward, although some folks do have difficultly in finding just where the holster is supposed to sit on their belt, which also must pass through their regular pants belt loops. (No moving of the belt loops lower on the body. Yes, we all recognize that women's builds and most holsters don't go together. But there are holster adapters that move the holster out away from the body and hol-

ster designs that do allow for strong-side carry and draw for women.)

From the IDPA rule book, "...The holster must position the pistol so the center line of the trigger pad is *behind* the centerline of the body from a side view and all magazines and magazine carriers for pistols must be *behind* the centerline. Revolver ammunition carriers may be worn directly in front of the holster on the strong side. The seam on the side of a shooters pants *may or may not* indicate where the centerline of a shooter's body is located.... (Emphasis added.) Only two magazine carriers may be worn." This rule is designed to keep "real-world" use at the forefront, since not many of us go about our daily lives with a complete belt full of spare ammo.

IDPA allows strong-side holsters only. Yes, the shoulder rig, crossdraw, small-of-the-back, ankle or whatever-else-carry may well be your normal mode of daily carry and quite practical (for you), but these rigs do not easily allow a safety comfort zone in a competitive environment. When a gun is drawn from these types of carry rigs, the gun muzzle may well sweep others on the range. Chances are, if you have a normal strong-side holster you will have no problem using your rig at an IDPA event. (And if you do have a problem, you can be sure someone will lend you the gear necessary to participate.)

If you own a handgun for self-defense and want to try your hand at shooting IDPA events, you probably already own most of the necessary gear. As I've mentioned, all you need is a standard handgun chambered for 9mm or above, a strong-side holster, three magazines or speed loaders and concealed carriers to tote them on your pants belt. The IDPA way is that everyone can compete using a shoot-straight-out-of-the-box or lightly-customized blaster of his or her choice in a concealed-carry holster. IDPA competitions are a place to test your gun-handling skills, not how "trick" you can make your gun to get a perceived or real edge over others. And, as I noted earlier, IDPA doesn't award prizes or money, only trophies. But, and there's always a but, we are a competitive bunch and some guns, calibers and holsters do

CHAPTER THREE ~ Get the Right Gear

Low walls and constricted firing ports present a challenge in this IDPA match stage.

work better for the game than others. In the Stock Service Pistol Division, the 9mm is the best cartridge, for you gain no competitive advantage (in fact you lose some) shooting a bigger, heavier-recoiling round. The Glock 9mm guns with the Safe-Action trigger are coming on as the choice over traditional double-action semi-autos, although a good man with a DA/SA gun can, and often does, win. For instance, at the 2000 National Championship, first place went to Ernest Langdon, who was shooting a 9mm Beretta Elite II, while David Sevigny trailed him by a hairbreadth difference in score using the 9mm Practical/Tactical Glock Model 34. In 2002, they changed finishes, with Sevigny finishing first and Langdon coming in second with the same guns. (Proving once again that it's the man, not the gun, that makes the difference.)

In Enhanced Service Pistol right now, the .38 Super 1911 is the "winning" gun. I think this combination is riding on top for two reasons. First, a fair number of the first group to join and shoot IDPA events already owned single-column, compensated .38 Super 1911s, lots of brass and reloading equipment. A quick trip to the gunsmith and the comp was gone – and the remaining gun was set up for the ESP Division. With years of R&D done in IPSC shooting, most everyone learned how to make the .38 Super caliber totally reliable in a 1911 gun. The 9mm round hasn't had this benefit, but with cheap factory 9mm creating interest in 9mm 1911s, the gunsmiths will quickly learn to make the 9mm 1911s run 100% of the time, I'm sure. (The guns do work with FMJ ammo, but not some JHPs, which can cause cartridge "jump," whereby the top round feeding from the mag tips or squirts up, trapping the extracting empty case and causing a very ugly jam.)

Custom Defensive Pistol Division is the home for the custom 1911 in .45ACP. This is the lair of John Browning's 1911. Here is where all the factory and custom 1911s are shot. (But any semi-auto chambered for the same caliber can be used in this division. For example, the Glock Model 21 in .45ACP can be shot in Stock Service Pistol or Custom Defensive Pistol.)

What is the winning gun? The 1911 in .45ACP is the current champ, with winners using guns from Springfield, Wilson, Kimber, Baer and Colt. The guns are allowed to have frame checkering, high-visibility sights (often night sights), extended safeties and are all more accurate than can possibly be needed for the match scenarios.

For Stock Service Revolver, any 4" or shorter-barreled revolver chambered for .38 Special and above can be used. I've seen Ruger Redhawks, Colt Pythons, the old reliable S&W Model 10, as well as S&W Model 66s with 2.5" barrel being shaken out over an IDPA course. The winning gun is the S&W Model 25 or Model 625 chambered for .45ACP (and .45 Auto Rim) and shot using full-moon clips to hold all six rounds together for reloading. With only a little practice, I find I reload one of these as quickly as I do a mag change on a 1911. (OK, I'm not a ball of fire with either one!) The kicker is that in this division, all revolver ammo, including the 10mm and the .45s, only has to meet the 125,000 power floor. This translates into being able to use really "wimp" loads if you choose to in the large-frame guns. (One further note on revolver ammo power floors: The ammo

CHAPTER THREE ~ Get the Right Gear

must meet the minimum power factor fired from a 4" revolver, but you can shoot these loads from a shorter-barreled gun without penalty.)

S&W has the Model 625 4"-barrel Mountain gun in .45ACP and .45 Colt, and has had runs of the Model 610 10mm revolver with 3" barrel. The S&W 610 is now being made with a 4" barrel length with IDPA as its intended mark.

If you shoot, you have to reload the gun somewhere in a course of fire. You can get by at a match with three mags or speedloaders, but it's a pain. Better to have six or more and a belt carrier for two of them. With the semi-auto mags, any mag pouch will do, but an open-top version that holds both mags with bullet noses forward and allows a full grip is best. Revolver speedloader carriers must be of the type that would be carried for self-defense use, not the competition speed loader carriers. The Shoot-the-Moon full-moon clip carriers are the ones the top guns use for their .45ACP wheel guns.

For the other revolvers, I use the HKS-brand clips because I'm most familiar with them, having used them on the job. As far as magazines go, buy the very best, factory-original. Don't settle for a gun show "$5 Special" to go with your $700 gun! And remember, you needn't use the expensive pre-ban mags for competition.

What holsters are the winners using? Most of the more well-known brands that really do conceal a handgun, be the rig built from leather, nylon, Kydex or plastic, with the nod going to the latter two as they are very quick. And be sure to get a *sturdy* gun belt to go with your holster and spare ammo carriers. (If you can crush the belt in your hand, it probably won't work. Gun belts are best obtained from holster makers, not a department store's men's accessories section.)

When you go to a shoot, there are some other items that will improve the quality of life for you. From top to bottom: You need a cap with a bill – facing front, please – and eye and ear protection. (The hat bill goes to the front to deflect empty cases from hitting you in the head or getting caught between your face and your shooting glasses. This hurts!) Let me emphasize these last two items. *Use wraparound, impact-resistant eye protection and a good set of ear protectors* – either muffs or plugs and preferably both – when anywhere on a firing range.

Trust me on this. (I know, run like hell when someone says that, but I'm as serious as a heart attack.) I have spent most of my life behind a gun: in the U.S. Army, U.S. Secret Service, the Philadelphia Fugitive Unit, teaching shooters and testing guns. Guns are my job and my passion. Thanks to gunfire, I'm partially deaf. Not going – I'm already there. My right ear went when a fellow soldier failed to clear a live round of .30 caliber from his

This IDPA stage required competitors to shoot while backing up.

M1 while he was standing at port arms to my right. He fired with the muzzle pointed over my head and sent my right ear into a cone of silence.

CHAPTER THREE ~ *Get the Right Gear*

And over the ensuing years, I've had a couple of guns fired past my head, again always on the right side, adding to the ear damage. Add to that years of not using any, or using inadequate, ear protection and tinnitus (ringing in the ears) has become my Muzak of daily living. So, like I said...get industry-rated wrap-around specs, and double plug – preferably using electronic muffs. You just might avoid having to answer everyone with, "Huh"?

As for my eyes, yes, I still have both, but only thanks to divine providence. I've been hit in my left eye twice with back splatter and I've lost count of the number of times I've been hit on my glasses and on my face. Bullet back-splatter occurs from dirt berms traveling back as far as 25 yards and even to 50 yards if steel targets or rocks are hit.

Next, wear a long-sleeve shirt if at all tolerable. The long sleeves protect you from back splatter of the rounds going down range and really help if you go prone. I also strongly recommend long pants with enough room in the legs so that you can wear knee pads beneath them. Jeans will work, but cargo pants are more comfortable, with Royal Robbins being the current "in" label. On my feet, I like ankle-length leather boots for support. (Mine are Danner brand.) IDPA courses aren't track meets, so you can skip the snazzy running shoes. Insect repellant and sun screen are often must-have items as well.

Finally, you need a good range bag. Range bags are like closets; get one bigger than you think you'll need, because you'll fill it quickly with gun, ammo, eye and ear protection and spare mags. You might well bring a range rod (for removing that embarrassing squib load – from the other guy's gun, of course). Also add a pen, screwdrivers, gun oil, sun screen, adhesive bandages (this is for the guy who *didn't* wear long pants and a long-sleeve shirt), snacks, water and maybe a fold-up rain poncho. With all this gear, you should be good to go. Oh, and don't forget to get a progressive reloading press; you'll need it if you like the game.

CHAPTER FOUR

Shoot in All Divisions to Gain and Maintain Proficiency with Various Types of Handguns

I've briefly touched on the types and calibers of the handguns used in IDPA competition in the first three chapters. The choices are many but uncomplicated, and need not be expensive. An IDPA member can use any center-fire semi-auto or double-action revolver chambered for calibers .38 Special (.355) and up (with a barrel length of 4" or less) and yes, if you were so inclined, you could use a single-action revolver.

IDPA is where you can use your self-defense handgun, be it any one of the popular double-action/single-action pistols such as the Beretta, Taurus, Smith & Wesson semi-auto, SIG Arms or Glock. Any good-quality miliary surplus arm would also be satisfactory. Or you can dust off your old S&W 4" barrel Model 19 revolver or fire up a large-frame .45 caliber version. If you've gotten the 1911 bug and have a custom defensive 1911, there's a place for that, too.

The way the matches are set up in the divisions previously mentioned, almost any self-defense handgun competes on a level playing field. Each action type competes in its own class and, at the club level, the BUG class is for snub noses and the mini semi-autos. (Although the minimum bore diameter rules applies here, too, I would think that the local match officials would allow the occasional .32, .25 or .22 pocket auto.) You don't need and in fact, as I mentioned earlier, are prohibited from using a highly-customized, compensated, scoped and high-capacity 1911 and a trick gun-carrying system. (The very-good-for-their-purpose speed rigs can't be considered carry holsters by any stretch of the imagination.)

In addition, as IDPA scenarios attempt to replicate "this-could-happen-to-me" events, the scenarios don't require the firing of 40 gazillion rounds to complete the stage. (That is, unless you are an extremely poor shot!) IDPA rules specifically target the elimination of "run and gun" stages, with the rules limiting rounds fired on a stage to a maximum of 18 with a few extra rounds allowed on occasion. To also keep scenarios within the bounds of realism, the longest shot is strongly suggested to be no further than 15 yards and the number of no-shoot targets in the scenario is mandated to be in the ratio of one no-shoot to every three shoot targets.

To evaluate the guns of IDPA, I chose the 1999 IDPA National Championship held at Lake Cormorant, Mississippi. It had a representative sampling of the types of guns and gear that might be found at an IDPA event, for equipment rules were evenly and completely enforced.

We begin with the Standard Service Pistol Division, where Tom Yost came in first shooting a Smith & Wesson Performance Center S&W Model 5906 chambered in 9mm. His gear was a Blade-Tech Concealex holster and he used Cor-Bon Tactical 9mm factory ammo. Rob Haught, a police chief in Sisterville, West Virginia and a member of the Beretta-sponsored factory team, took second in SSP with a Beretta 92 Elite in 9mm with a Blade-Tech rig and Cor-Bon 9mm Tactical ammo. Following closely on his teammate's heels, Ernest Langdon, also on the Beretta shooting team, was third with, what else, a Beretta 92 Elite, Blade-Tech paddle rig and Cor-Bon Tactical 9mm.

A Smith & Wesson N-frame 3"-barrel revolver in custom leather.

CHAPTER FOUR ~ Shoot in All Divisions

Moving to the next class, Enhanced Service Pistol, FBI Special Agent Scott Warren took first place with a Springfield 1911 chambered in .40S&W in a Wilson Combat Tactical Assault holster and his own home-brewed .40 ammo done on a Dillon 1050. Brice Linskey used a Performance Center 9mm Model 5906, a Blade-Tech holster and Cor-Bon 9mm to come in right behind Scott, while John Sayle stuck with his decades-old Wilson Custom .38 Super 1911, Wilson Rapid Response holster and his own handloads to take third place.

Moving up to the full-house big-bore guns used in the Custom Defensive Pistol Division, Bill Wilson ran at the front of the pack with a Wilson CQB .45ACP, a Wilson Combat Practical Holster and handloads. Gregory Martin followed using a Norinco(!) 1911 in .45ACP worked over by Wilson Combat and drawn from a Wilson Tactical rig shooting handloads. John McGuire took some time out from his duty of Safety Officer running stages at the Nationals to take third place with a Colt 1911 in .45ACP with his own custom work, drawn from a Milt Sparks Executive Companion holster using handloads.

The revolver guys mostly used S&Ws. Alex Zimmermann took first with an S&W Model 625 in .45ACP, a Ky-Tac rig and handloads; Dave Jackson used the same gun for second place with a High Desert Talon holster and handloads; and Morgan Dague, third, also chose an S&W Model 625, the High Desert Talon Tactical R4 holster and handloads to make the Trifecta complete.

Now, it gets interesting when the equipment survey is studied. From the top, Glock rang up an impressive total of 52 listings – Models 17, 19, 21, 22, 23, 30, 34 and 35 in 9mm, .40S&W and .45ACP. Smith & Wesson had a total of 34 guns in the event. The semi-autos included Models 3913, 5906, 59 and CQB; the S&W revolvers were Models 15, 19, 586, 686, 66, 67, 610 and 625 in .38 Special to .45ACP. Beretta semi-autos numbered 12, with four

Browning High-Power in a Kydex holster.

Model 92s, seven Beretta Elites and one DA-only Model 96 in 9mm and .40 calibers. SIG Arms had 10 guns in .357 SIG, 9mm, .40 and .45ACP. Heckler & Koch had eight guns – the USP, P7 and P9 in 9mm, .40S&W and .45ACP. Three CZ-75 selective DA/SA guns in 9mm were tallied, as were two Ruger semi-autos, a P89 and 95, both in 9mm. Tanfoglio had one high-cap .40 CZ-type pistol, along with a single Taurus 9mm PT911 and a .40-caliber Walther P99, while a Kahr P9 9mm semi-auto also made a solo appearance (this had to be a die-hard tactical man!). Two fine Colt Python revolvers in .357 Magnum also were brought out of mothballs for the match.

In 1911s, Colt led the pack with 31 1911s in .45, .40, .38 Super and 9mm. Kimber and Wilson Combat tied with 20 competitors each. Springfield followed closely with 13 of its 1911s in 9mm, .40 and .45ACP. Para-Ordnance had nine guns chambered for the 9mm, .40 and .45ACP. Les Baer guns tallied six in the same calibers, tying with Nowlin Manufacturing 1911s in 9mm and .45ACP. Two Caspian 1911s ran, as well as a .40S&W high-cap STI/SVI.

The other interesting bit of information from the shooters' equipment survey is the brands and quantities of concealment holsters. The big numbers went to Blade-Tech with 69, followed by 38 Wilson Combat rigs, 16 Safariland designs, 15 from Dillon, 12 Ky-Tac holsters, 12 from Galco and 11 from Hellweg. Sparks almost made the double-digit column with nine rigs, with single entries going to Alessi, Bears Den, Bev McCord, Bianchi, Del Fatti, DeSantis, Don Hume, FIST, Fobus, Glock, Gunsite, Heinie, Hill, John May, Kramer, Mad-Dog, Mike Benedict, Rosen, PWI, Springbok, Talon, Tactical Tools, Uncle Mike's, Vega and Wild Bill's. A wide range of gear and names well-known to handgun self-defense users, certainly, but many are names not found on the usual "practical" handgun circuit.

Also, 75 custom gunsmiths were listed, with 13 guns worked on

CHAPTER FOUR ~ Shoot in All Divisions

by their owners. Reloading presses included Dillon, Hornady, Lee, RCBS, Lyman and Star. (This last is a name not seen for awhile, but a press that obviously lasts forever!)

Most of us who shoot in IDPA events would agree that we're interested in gaining and maintaining proficiency with our defensive handgun. Now, here's the rub. If you're only shooting with one action type and caliber you're neglecting your education. You should be proficient with as many types of defensive arms as possible and, within the range of IDPA handgun divisions, there are enough varying guns to choose from sufficient for you to be assured of some level of competency with most of the common action types. In fact, IDPA offers an achievement award when a member is equally classified in all four divisions.

Glock model 36 in a Del Fatti concealment rig.

For example, select a Beretta or a SIG pistol for Stock Service Pistol. For Enhanced Service Pistol, get a 9mm or .38 Super 1911 and then you can transition over to Custom Defensive Pistol with a 1911 chambered for the .45ACP. You obviously need a wheel gun for Revolver Division, but everyone should own a Model 19, so no big deal. If you want to avoid buying and using three separate semi-autos, you can shoot Stock Service Pistol with a gun that has selective double- and single-action carry such as the CZ and its clones. This same gun then could be shot in Enhanced Service Pistol and, if it were chambered for .45ACP, you could stretch and shoot it in Custom Defensive pistol with the same cocked-and-locked start you use in the Enhanced Service Pistol Division. Another suggestion would be to get a Glock Model 21 in .45ACP. This is okay for both Stock Service Pistol and Custom Defensive Pistol. You'll only need one other semi-auto and a wheel gun this way.

For your efforts at getting this four-division classification, you'll gain a couple of things. First off, you'll shoot a lot more and learn to shoot better – and that can't hurt. Second, you will learn the strengths and weaknesses of the various action types. (You'll be surprised to find while doing this that many of the commonly-held beliefs about the various guns are not correct.)

As a reward for your work, in addition to personal satisfaction, you can get a certificate, a plaque and listing on the IDPA website to recognize your achievement. Simply send your scores and $40 to the IDPA office. You can be noted as a Four-Gun Marksman, Sharpshooter, Expert or Master – a formal "bragging rights" type of thing.

Curiously, there was, in the dark and distant past of Practical Shooting, a Combat Master Award. A few very deserving pistoleros earned and were honored with the title, but the mechanism and the title have fallen by the wayside. (Those who have the title are justifiably proud of it, however.) Now, IDPA will not elevate you to Combat Master, but if you can shoot Master scores on the IDPA classifier in all four divisions, you're a long way along to being a very capable... well, combat master.

As I mentioned earlier, there is also a fifth division authorized for use only at the local club match level, the Back-Up Gun (BUG) Division, that is not recognized at state or national events. The BUG segment is a great way to find out just how well, or not, you can handle your favorite back-up gun.

Paraphrasing from the IDPA rulebook, the handguns permitted in the Back-up Gun Division may be single- or double-action, either pistol or revolver; must be in .32 auto, .380 ACP, 9x19mm, .38 Special, .357 magnum, .40S&W, 10mm or .45 ACP; and must meet the following criteria: Semi-autos can only have a maximum barrel length of 3.8" or less, factory cone barrels with or without a barrel bushing are allowed, revolvers are limited to 3" or shorter barrels, and all BUG Division guns must be loaded with no more than five rounds. Permitted modifications to the

CHAPTER FOUR ~ Shoot in All Divisions

A Glock Model 35, good for use in IDPA's Standard Service Pistol Division and for personal defense.

guns follow those listed for their big brothers in Stock Service Pistol and Stock Service Revolver Divisions. A good read of these rules shows that you can shoot a pretty wide range of so-called back-up guns in the BUG Division, from the diminutive DA .32 autos up to a .44 mag 3"-barrel revolver.

For those who want a real challenge, the Smith & Wesson five shooters, the airweight and magnum-loaded frames and the Seecamp, North American Arms, Beretta and Kel-Tec .32s would be the guns on the line. For those who do carry a bigger second gun, the wheel gun choices would be the K- and L-frames from Taurus and S&W in .357 Magnum, 10mm, .41 Magnum, .44 Magnum, and .45 Colt. And if you want a real challenge, get a single-action Colt-type gun and go to it.

If your taste runs to semi-autos, the field is almost without limit, for just about every concealable semi-auto qualifies in this class. The line between a BUG gun and what is normally chosen for a primary gun is easily blurred, because many use these subcompacts as their primary defense arm. This disparity of sizes is one good reason why the BUG class isn't a national-level event. It would quickly get gamed out, with most everyone using a short 1911 or a Glock or the .357 S&W Model 66, shooting .38s, or the now-discontinued .38 Special-chambered Model 15 with 2" barrel.

Another game gun would be the S&W Model 610 that had a limited run with a 3" barrel, since with this you could use full-moon clips for a very quick reload. Of course, all this defeats the intended purpose of the BUG class, which is to give local cubs a venue to attract and interest shooters in becoming proficient with their defensive arms. Shooting a local match with your arm of choice could well be an eye-opener, for some of the little guns are damned hard to use well unless you practice with them– and no, carrying one every day doesn't cut it as practice.

One final note: Since the mode of carry for these guns varies widely, most clubs would do well to have the shooter start with the gun off-body, say on a table or in a drawer. This would eliminate any time-consuming discussion of types of holsters or safe alternative methods of drawing the gun.

CHAPTER FOUR ~ *Shoot in All Divisions*

A Wilson CQB Compact .45 and Wilson gear, a good choice for self-defense or IDPA's Custom Defensive Pistol Division.

CHAPTER FIVE
Concealed – Carry Draw

Given the generally-practical nature of IDPA courses of fire, a concealed-carry draw usually begins the stage. This draw stroke differs from that used for an open-carry draw.

I suggest you develop one concealed-carry draw that allows you to consistently and reflexively move the covering garment out of the way so that you get a good shooting grip on your gun and are able to move the gun to the target without any chance of its getting tied up in your coat. There are any number of methods to do this.

The one I use is to bring the back edge of my opened shooting hand to center line on my body and sweep my coat back past the holstered gun and then come forward and down onto the gun. At the same time, I bring my off-hand up to center line, at the ready to meet my shooting hand/gun. (See photos on next page.) This is not the quickest draw but, for me, is the most positive. An alternative and faster technique is to sweep your coat back just far enough to get your gun hand beneath the gun and, on the way up, "snatch" the gun out, in effect pulling the gun into your hand as it (your hand) goes by. This method is fast but it leaves me open to missing the gun or not getting a good grip.

Now, as to the covering garment. In yesteryear (it has been a very long time), there was a notion that you should always keep coins, spare ammo or even stones in your gun-side coat pocket, the idea being that a weighted coat will stay back and give you more time to get to your gun before the coat swings forward. Another method was (trust me, we did do this at one point) to grab the hemline of your coat on the off side and then raise that same arm, pulling the coat off and back behind the gun. This works but assumes you have the room to wave your arm and that the coat doesn't snag on or drag your gun out of the holster.

The new "trick of the moment" is to put a plastic flex cuff in the front gun-side edge (the seam) of your photojournalist vest. This, I've been somberly informed, was "developed by the State Department Diplomatic Security guys." OK, instead of stones we are now building a corset. (For anyone who doesn't know what this is, ask your grandfather.) This may well be great for a game, but are we really going to flex-cuff all our coats?

If you're interested in developing a real practical skill, ask yourself..."does it work with almost all clothing?" (Some materials cling more than others and can be death traps if used for gun concealment.) Now, I admit to a bias. I think the whole notion of a fast-draw defense is overrated. I've only had to use a "fast draw" about a dozen times in my lifetime and in more than half of them, I should have seen the problem coming. The adage of "smooth is quick" is the key to a good draw for IDPA or for self-defense. I would advise you to find one that doesn't require a martial arts dance to execute!

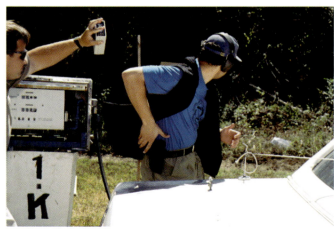

Two examples of concealed-carry draws being used during IDPA match stages.

CHAPTER FIVE ~ *Concealed-Carry Draw*

Author demonstrates the proper steps for a good concealed-carry draw: Get your covering garment clear of the gun and then establish your shooting grip while your gun is still in the holster.

An example of the beginning of a good concealed-carry draw. Duane Long, left, makes sure his vest is well clear of the gun before he attempts to continue the draw.

CHAPTER SIX
Strong- and Weak-Hand Shooting

The IDPA Classifier CL-0001 tests, among other skills, your ability to shoot multiple targets with both single and multiple rounds while only using your strong hand, unsupported, for segments of the course of fire. This one-hand use of a handgun is a skill that is necessary for both IDPA competition and real-world self-defense.

There are basically two ways of firing a gun one-handed. The first, and the most efficient in terms of quickly getting a round into the threat and not telegraphing your intent, is to simply draw and fire without changing your stance – hopefully without any body movement not directly connected to the physical act of drawing and firing. (If you move your head and/or shoulders, you telegraph the direction in which you intend to move.) This is very quick and effective for close-range work, say five yards and closer. It is not as strong for follow-up shots as is the second and more widely-taught technique. Call the first the QD (Quick and Dirty) and the second the AF (Aim and Fire).

In the AF, as you draw the gun you step forward with your strong-side foot, shift your weight forward on this foot and turn toward the target; lean into the gun, as it were. In addition to these movements, you should immobilize your non-shooting arm by either stiffening it so that it is locked at your side or locked across your body. Doing this will also tighten up your back and shoulder muscles, which makes for a very strong stance in which you can much better control the gun for multiple shots. Both techniques need to be mastered, as it's rare that targets are conveniently positioned so that you can use the second, more aggressive shooting platform. More likely, the target or threat is off to one side or the other.

In the IDPA Classifier CL-0001, emphasis is more on accuracy over speed, with the targets at seven and ten yards, so the AF

An aggressive stance helps control recoil when shooting with one hand.

shooting stance is the better choice, particularly because there is no movement required after firing one and then two shots on each of three targets.

The strong stance also lends itself to sighted fire, since your arm is fully extended and your gun is raised to eye level. In the QD method, you can fire your gun at any time along the draw stroke, with or without the use of sights, since the gun itself is used for alignment with the target.

The IDPA Classifier also requires one-handed shooting using your less-dominant or "weak" hand. In the Classifier, you start with the gun in your off-hand, lowered to a 45-degree angle from the target. Any manual safeties may be disengaged prior to the start signal.

CHAPTER SIX ~ Strong- and Weak-Hand Shooting

Shifting your weight forward, leaning into the gun and tensing your off hand, arms and back muscles increases stability and produces better recoil control.

For "Quick and Dirty" work, simply shoot without any additional body movement.

When we designed this classifier at the IDPA Founding Meeting, the consensus was this start position eliminated the need for a weak-hand draw, the execution of which had come to be viewed as inherently unsafe. (Not true if properly done, but things can get really exciting if the draw is fumbled!)

Weak-hand shooting is a mirror image of the strong-side position. If you want to use your sights, the quickest way to use them, considering that most right-handed shooters are right-eye dominant, is to move the gun toward your body's center line to minimize, if not eliminate, head and eye movement. Since you begin this stage with the gun in your hand, you should use a strong shooting stance, with your gun-side (weak-hand) leg forward and your weight shifted onto it – in effect leaning into the gun. As with the strong-hand-only shooting platform, you should immobilize your non-shooting arm by bringing it up to the center line of your body and stiffening it or simply stiffening it as it hangs along your side.

Since a handgun recoils away from its strongest support and assuming, for purposes of illustration, you're holding the gun in your left hand, you should consider shooting multiple targets from left to right because the gun will be moving up and to the right after the shot is fired. (The reverse should be done with the gun in your right or strong hand.)

CHAPTER SEVEN ~ *One-Hand and Retention Shooting*

CHAPTER SEVEN
One-Hand and Retention Shooting

As we've noted, in IDPA a contestant is often asked to fire his handgun one-handed. Most times this is either strong-hand-only or weak-hand-only, as we discussed in Chapter Six. There is a third, less-used position – "from retention." There seems to be some confusion about exactly what the retention position requires. On page 64 of the IDPA Course of Fire book is Course Number SS-003 titled, **"A Buy Gone Bad,"** which is also illustrated in Chapter Sixteen (pages 54 and 55) of this handbook. In as much as I designed and submitted this course of fire (based on an actual incident), let me explain what I mean by "retention," and the real-world need for it.

Picture this. You have gone to a bar with an informant to meet two brothers who are looking to sell some counterfeit money. You enter the bar. The bar proper is on your right and booths line the left wall. You pick a booth about fifteen feet in from the door. The informant slides into the bench seat first and is up against the wall. The seat faces the door and you get in next to him. He's on your right side. The two brothers fill up the opposite seats. You are situated so that you can see them, the door behind them and your partner, who is seated at the bar on your left.

You spend some time haggling about who has what. You want to be sure they have the counterfeit money and they want to find out if you were dumb enough to have the buy money on your person. If you brought the money, chances are the bad guys will rip you off rather than sell you the merchandise. By robbing you, they can then use the same goods to re-bait the "hook" for another customer. Worst case, they have to sell the product.

After a good bit of back and forth questioning, you are exasperated and at an impasse and, wanting to do the deal (after a few of these, you learn to walk away rather than push it), you tell them yes, you have the money with you. (Remember, too, you are with an informant. If he's willing to sell them out, he'll also sell you out.) Upon hearing this, they say they have a gun under the table and that you should give them the money. You decide that this is not a good thing and draw your weapon to take care of business. Now, if you're seated in a cramped, high-backed booth with two guys who say they want to rob you and you have an informant on your right, how far away from your body would the gun be when you draw it in these circumstances? Right! You'd hold the gun back against your chest with one hand and tilt it slightly outboard so that it wouldn't snag on your clothing and thus could cycle properly. That's the retention position!

In the retention position, the gun is held close to your body and turned or canted away slightly to allow the slide to cycle.

CHAPTER SEVEN ~ *One-Hand and Retention Shooting*

Ray Coffman demonstrates the classic retention position to a class at Thunder Ranch.
Top photo shows the draw, bottom photo the result.

CHAPTER EIGHT
Engaging Targets – In Priority and/or Sequence

Rob Haught shoots threats in Tactical Priority.

Some of the IDPA lingo is a bit confusing to a first-time shooter. The terms "Tactical Priority" and "Tactical Sequence" are two that get many competitors unnecessary penalties. (IDPA members call these "Procedurals," meaning you didn't do something correctly.)

According to the IDPA rule book, *Tactical Priority* means that you shoot the targets in the order of the threat presented. This most often simply means shoot the close ones (targets) first and the farthest away last if, and only if, the targets are separated from each other by more than two yards, the logic being the closest opponent to you is most probably the biggest threat. (There must be a minimum distance of two yards between targets for the Tactical Priority rule to be applied.)

Tactical Priority should not be confused with the proper use of cover, wherein you shoot the first target you see as you come out from behind the cover. This first target can be, and often is, farther away than the others in the array, but it's a case of "who you see first gets served first!"

OK, Tactical Priority is understandable, but what then is *Tactical Sequence*? This requirement is found in the IDPA classifier, where you are told how many shots to fire at each target and in what order to do it. The thinking is that when facing multiple targets, each target gets one round before you re-engage any of them. The rule book example suggests three targets to be shot. You would fire 1-1-2-1-1...one each in target number one and target number two, and then two rounds into target number three; then go back to target number one or two with one round. This translates into "everyone gets served before anyone get seconds." I personally question if anyone is going to have the presence of mind to only fire one shot in a real-world confrontation; but then again, if you only have a five-shooter such as a J-frame S&W, it would be prudent to be able to manage your ammunition capacity.

Tacticians can debate if this is a viable defense technique or not. Suffice to say that this is an IDPA shooting challenge with possible real-world application. I would hope that no one would combine the two requirements into one course of fire, for each should be addressed and performed on its own for the shooter to get any benefit from the exercise.

Tactical Sequence - one round on each target and repeat.

CHAPTER EIGHT ~ *Engaging Targets – In Priority and/or Sequence*

In this scenario, whatever target your gun covers first gets shot first, because the targets are not separated by two yards.

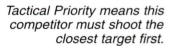

Tactical Priority means this competitor must shoot the closest target first.

These targets are more than two yards apart, so the closest one gets shot first – for "tactical priority."

• • • 37 • • •

CHAPTER NINE
Shooting on the Move

In IDPA competition, as is the case in a real-world application, shooting on the move is a necessary skill to develop and perfect. In IDPA shoots, the courses of fire often require movement to and from positions of cover or concealment. (Per the IDPA rule book, all movement in a stage should not be more than ten yards.)

While moving from cover, targets are offered for engagement and, since scoring is based on both points-on-target and time, shooting on the run rather than stopping to engage saves time and betters your score. This dynamic mode of firing is also a good self-defense skill – provided you can hit when you're in motion. In IDPA and in real life, suppressive fire is the province of only the military, not the legally-armed citizen!

There are a few ways to shoot on the move – some bad and some better than others. Simply walking or running upright while firing doesn't give good hits unless you're at arm's length from the target, for your arms and gun move in mirror motion to your stride as you push off and land on the ground. The "Groucho" walk, named after comedian Groucho Marx, is an exaggerated crouch with the shooter's back arched forward. (It's better seen than described.) This shooting platform is stable but very tiring if done for any length of time (not the case in a competition, of course). So the "Groucho" walk has fallen out of favor with law enforcement trainers and operators because of the fatigue involved.

Another method of shooting on the move is the "drag step," where you advance one big step and then drag the trailing leg up to your new location and repeat. This can be done quite quickly and is very stable. The downside is that you're making noise with your dragging leg and if the ground is uneven, the dragged foot can catch on the ground itself or on debris.

A better method, for me, is a heel-to-toe walk, knees slightly bent and my feet moving as if they were straddling a center line. At no time is either foot directly in front of the other as is the case when walking normally. I particularly like this one because, regardless of where I am in the "walk," I have the ability to immediately change direction.

The way I teach movement shooting is to have the student hold a cup of water filled almost to the brim and then have him move toward and away from the targets holding the cup and admonish him not to spill the water. I also give him the mental imagery that the cup holds hot coffee. This seems to work quite well; everyone relates to not wanting to scald their hands.

The object remains, of course, to get hits. But also, in a real-world application, you want to get as much distance between you and the threat as you can – as quickly as you can. So if you practice these techniques, work both for the competitive game and personal defense by picking up the pace as soon as you get good hits.

Kathie Rauch engages targets to the left while advancing downrange at Blackwater's "Steel Alley," with Chris Edwards coaching.

CHAPTER NINE ~ Shooting on the Move

Author uses a slight knee bend while moving forward and shooting at a target. Movement should be done from the waist down, keeping the upper body as level and steady as possible.

Scott Warren moves forward and to the right with a slight crouch.

Putting it in "reverse," the shooting platform is the same.

Frank James, left, and Chris Edwards shoot on the move at a training class at Thunder Ranch.

• • • 39 • • •

CHAPTER TEN

Using Cover and "Slicing the Pie"

As we discussed in previous chapters, one of the principles of IDPA is to provide shooters with practical and realistic courses of fire that simulate a potentially life-threatening encounter or test skills required in such an eventuality. Two skills you must possess is the ability to shoot from behind hard and soft cover. The rule has in mind a vertical barricade and the ability to "pie" the corner.

Since IDPA is a sport and not a tactical training event, IDPA rules, as we pointed out earlier, generously mandate that you only need to keep more than 50% of your upper torso and *all* of the remainder of your body behind the barricade when firing or looking for targets. This generous requirement allows for many variations in techniques and is certainly not the best use of cover, as would be done in a threatening real-life situation, but it does reinforce the fact that proper use of cover is absolutely necessary for self-defense applications.

Using the "+50" rule, a competitor should position himself, if at all possible, well back from the barricade or cover and engage the targets as he sees them. Staying back from cover helps the shooter remain covered or protected behind the barricade while making it easier to safely locate and engage the targets. Generally, the closer you are to a barricade, the more of you needs to be exposed so that you can find and shoot the target array.

For self-defense most of the above rules are still applicable, although you are best served by only allowing your gun muzzle and one eye to come out from behind cover. This would be done in a slow, deliberate manner, for any quick movement draws attention to your position. Also, by taking your time you may eliminate bumping into or stepping on things that make noise – another great target indicator.

The IDPA rule of only engaging targets as you see them goes hand-in-hand with the +50 rule. This is generally referred to as "pieing the corner" or "slicing the pie," which describes deliberately sectioning the area to be viewed for a threat. You expose only enough of yourself from behind your cover so that you just take a single "slice" of the "pie." In effect, you visually cut the area that contains the targets to be engaged into sections, just as you would cut up a pie to be served, hence the term "pieing."

The two rules work together, so if the competitor moves out to be able to see more than one target in a three-target array, he is judged to be violating the +50 rule. One of the Safety Officers officiating on the stage ideally positions himself behind the competitor so that he sees both the shooter and the targets and can make a valid call on the shooter's observance of the +50 rule or assess him a penalty for non-compliance. IDPA Safety Officer courtesy is to yell "cover" if the rule is violated and if this warning is practical. (The shooter can be moving so quickly that he has repeatedly violated the rule before any notice can be given. In this case the penalty is applied.) The "warning" is not mandatory. The +50 behind cover is a fair means of assessing penalties for non-compliance in a sporting venue and most Safety Officers resolve any questions of these IDPA rules in favor of the shooter.

Good use of cover.

As to the actual use of pieing a corner, the real application might well be to take in much more of the threat area than is permitted in IDPA. I want to see as many threats as I can as quickly as I can with as little risk to me as possible *before* dealing with them. It would be fatal if the nearest threat to you is your last slice of the pie. You would, under IDPA rules, never have seen him and he would have watched as you dealt with the first and/or subsequent threats. Thus he would be ideally informed and situated to harm you.

CHAPTER TEN ~ Using Cover and "Slicing the Pie"

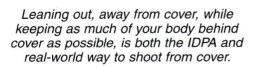

Leaning out, away from cover, while keeping as much of your body behind cover as possible, is both the IDPA and real-world way to shoot from cover.

• • • 41 • • •

CHAPTER ELEVEN
Low Cover/Kneeling

From the IDPA rule book dated May 5, 1999, "..The answer to solve the problem of using a low-cover position is to require the shooter to *have at least one knee on the ground* when actually firing."

The problem addressed by this rule is that if barricades and range props are included in a stage, the intent is that they be correctly used. Many shooters will approach a low barricade, say a barrel, squat, fire and move. A number of defensively-well-trained competitors disagree with the IDPA knee-on-the-ground rule, for they are able to just squat and still use the cover provided. The problem lies in administering penalties for improper use of cover. If the shooter moves quickly, he's down and back up, leaving a question as to whether he did in fact use the cover provided, keeping in mind that IDPA scenarios attempt to replicate real defense problems, albeit in an artificial environment.

Practical shooting requires practical shooting positions and practical shooting competition requires a level playing field, one in which the scoring officials are able to easily determine if the competitor is complying with all course requirements.

The founders of IDPA, veterans of practical shooting competitions, know how rules are misapplied and how they are sometimes "bent" by competitors seeking that little extra edge to win. The founders all have trained at one or more of the defensive firearms academies and some are well-known defensive firearms trainers in their own right. They are well aware of the tools needed to survive an armed encounter.

Given that IDPA shoots are competitive venues and the need to create and maintain a level playing field with consistent and fair calls by range officials is paramount, the mandate of one knee on the ground was established to obviate almost all need for a judgement call by range officials during a competition.

Along with this rule comes the inevitable reality of infirmaties and age. Prior knee injuries and the onslaught of time means that some can kneel more quickly than others, as would also be the case if squatting were permitted. IDPA has tried to make the competitive life as fair as possible, but no one claims to be a miracle worker.

Along with the requirement for kneeling comes the use of knee pads. IDPA, in an attempt to maintain the perception of reality, states that any knee pads, excluding orthopedic and other medically-prescribed braces, be worn beneath the pants. Course designers are also strongly encouraged to insure that the kneeling area is free from objects that might cause injury and to provide sufficient padding to the area if necessary.

IDPA rules require one knee on the ground when using low cover, but no one will fault you for using this more-stable shooting position.

In taking a kneeling position, a shooter can use one or both knees, kneel erect or squat back on one or both legs, creating a semi-seated, very low and stable shooting position. The ideal kneeling setup is one in which cover is properly used yet allows the shooter to quickly move, if necessary, to another shooting position.

CHAPTER ELEVEN ~ Low Cover/Kneeling

Various kneeling positions are used by, counterclockwise from top right, author; Walter M. Rauch; Kerby Smith; Chris Edwards; Everett Spear; Scott Warren; and author again.

• • • 43 • • •

CHAPTER TWELVE ~ Seated Shooting Positions

CHAPTER TWELVE
Seated Shooting Positions/ Chairs and Vehicles

Since most of us lead a sedentary life – that is, bluntly put, we spend altogether too much time on our butts – some of the IDPA courses of fire attempt to mimic our everyday living and you may find yourself seated in your favorite "couch potato" position and asked to shoot threats.

In most cases, you'll be seated in a straight-back chair without arm rests, but as shown in one of the accompanying photos, some inventive match directors provide you with a "real" chair, a recliner complete with faux channel changer, although most stage designers skip holding the obligatory beverage.

Drawing from a chair or any seated position, you must be muzzle conscious and not have the loaded gun pass over any part of your anatomy. Often in a chair stage, you are simply asked to retrieve your gun from a table along side or in front of you and all you have to do is pick it up safely.

If the course of fire requires you to get out of the chair, be careful that your spare magazines, your now-empty holster and any other items on your belt or attached to your pockets (the obligatory Spyderco knife, for example) don't get caught in the chair uprights or the chair's arms. Of course, when this happens your fellow competitors, spectators and Safety Officers are treated to the sight of a grown man trying to shoot or move with a chair attached to his body – sort of like a dysfunctional turtle!

If you are going to get out of the chair to continue the course of fire, you need to think about what you are going to do and how. Some shooters like a very explosive exit from the chair. This is quite tactically correct, but take care that you don't knock the chair over such that its legs go forward between *your* legs!

Some shooters like to grab the chair with their off-hand and throw it out of the way. This is pretty much an unnecessary, time-consuming and hazardous-to-others move. If necessary, because of your size and a light chair, just use your off-hand to stabilize the chair and save the chair toss for the movies. (Although IDPA range rules pretty much discourage any walk-through of the course of fire, most match directors and safety officers should let you try your "seat" first – for safety's sake.)

Of course, in IDPA scenarios you will eventually find yourself sitting behind the wheel of some sort of very old and beaten up

CHAPTER TWELVE ~ Seated Shooting Positions

car that isn't going anywhere. As you look out of the windshield and windows, you'll find yourself surrounded by threatening targets. Yes, you get to shoot from a car – our second homes.

Shooting from inside a car requires some attention, for drawing and shooting can be *very* exciting if your gun muzzle sweeps your legs or other treasured parts of your body! Since you are normally sitting behind the steering wheel, and if the targets are off to your left and you're right-handed, the quickest way to get to the targets is a line between the holstered gun and the targets – right across your body. This may well be the quickest and you'll probably do this if confronted with a real threat, but in a shooting event, discretion should be the better part of valor. IDPA HQ strongly discourages course designers from having anyone draw while seated in a car, although it is not prohibited. My opinion is that it should be done so that the more cautious will not lose out to the more daring or stupid.

While moving the gun from your hip to the target, it is also all too easy to catch the gun muzzle and front sight on the steering wheel. This can cause the gun to do a few things, none of which are good. It can simply fire when it is abruptly halted. Catching the gun on the steering wheel can also lever the gun down and take it out of your hand. Now, when someone accidentally drops something the normal reaction is to grab it. If this is done with a gun that is now pointing south, you will be fortunate if all you do is shoot the car!

For car stages, the best answer is to start with the gun already in hand, muzzle depressed below the windows. No realism is lost and safety is *almost* assured. (Murphy lives and anything that can go wrong will – at the most inopportune time.) Extend the gun and make sure your muzzle is clear of the car doors and then fire. (**NOTE:** There is a difference between having your sight clear and the gun muzzle clear. Make sure *both* the sight and the muzzle are clear before you fire.)

You may well need to reload inside the car. If you're wearing a coat, getting a spare mag is interesting. You can look like a squirrel digging for nuts doing this. By the way, be careful if you drop a mag or speedloader on the car floor. Odds are, you'll step on it while getting out and find that the mag or loader acts like ice!

Getting out, remember to take the gun out of the open window if you have fired from this position and be very muzzle-conscious, for when you open the door, the window frame can trap your gun hand. Of course, you must be careful not to catch the gun or the sights on the window frame, either. And, if you must close the door, *keep your hands and gun out of the door frame.* Also, save the seat belt removal and drawing for training, when it can be done at your own pace.

Additional Tip: You might want to wear both ear muffs and ear plugs and use wraparound eye protection for this shooting. Guns are much noisier inside a car and wraparound eye protection is for the stuff that will spray around inside the car if your shot doesn't make it outside.

• • • 45 • • •

CHAPTER THIRTEEN
Going Prone

Firing from the prone position is (or should be) part and parcel of any practical shooting sport and anyone who shoots an IDPA match should expect to find himself on his belly or his side, firing at targets from a low port in a wall or from beneath some sort of vehicle. If you haven't shot from prone, you need to practice safely being able to get into it, fire, reload, then get up and move before "learning on the job," so to speak, at a match.

Right off, there's a safety concern, for you are going down to the ground with a loaded gun in your hand. You don't want to accidentally close your hand and fire the gun if you lose your balance, or dig the gun into the dirt, point it in an unsafe direction or even drop it. To add to something that appears rather simple, you may also have to reload while on the ground. This definitely needs to be practiced with an empty gun. You may well find that magazine or speed loader pouches that work while you're erect may not when your movements are restricted by the earth.

To go prone, it helps to break the movement down and go through it step-by-step in practice. First you need to locate the threat and plan your approach so that you're behind cover or are using as much cover as possible. Next, get the gun out and in front of you. On the way down to the ground, get your non-shooting hand out and down toward the ground to stop your downward movement. Be careful not to point the gun at any part of your body while doing this.

For me, I like to go down on my gun side; first my leg, then my torso. I *fold* myself down, as it were, taking the brunt of the increasing body weight on more and more of my body, while using my off-hand for support and control of my direction. My gun stays pointed toward the target as I'm going down. As the right side of my body gets to the ground, my left leg remains bent at the knee, which holds the left side of my body slightly off the ground. My off-hand comes over and picks up my gun hand. I can fire at any time during this movement. If the targets are close, I shoot as soon as I'm down. If the targets are far and the ground is solid beneath me, I roll flatter to the ground and push down with both hands if the ground surface allows, making the ground work as a third hand to support the gun.

Depending on youth and physical agility, you can speed this up. For me, I now favor the previously-described "building collapsing" method. I just speed it up a bit. My friend Bill Rogers popularized the "flying squirrel" technique when he shot the Bianchi Cup. This is very quick. Simply throw yourself forward and down, and fire when you hit the earth!

For some stages, you need to be able to get prone without extending yourself forward of a specific fault line for safety reasons. In a real-world application, you may find yourself going prone in a very confined area. Another problem can arise in this shooting position...the loss of protective equipment and learning that your hat brim can blind you. Your ear muffs can get knocked off, along with your shooting glasses, and your hat brim is usually too low. Depending on how you are placed on the ground, you now can't get to your mag pouches because you are lying on them (or they also jumped out from the impact).

One last safety note. In competition, do not draw or reholster from the prone position, because the gun muzzle will be pointed behind you, covering any and all who may be standing there. Better to put the safety on or decock the gun while prone. Then, while keeping your strong-side or holster-side knee on the ground, carefully holster the gun. Alternatively, come up to both knees and holster. If you hurt yourself or are winded, gently put the gun down on the ground with the muzzle down range, safeties applied or gun cleared, and then regain it once you are able to come to your knees; or ask the Safety Officer to assist you.

Now if the course of fire asks that you get up to move and engage more targets, your finger must be out of the trigger guard. Muzzle control is paramount. Practice your "get ups" with a safe and empty gun *a lot* before doing it "hot." (I would discourage course designers from requiring any movement after a prone position in a stage, for it is all too easy to slip or lose your balance when getting up, not to mention that you may have knocked yourself silly getting down!)

CHAPTER THIRTEEN ~ *Going Prone*

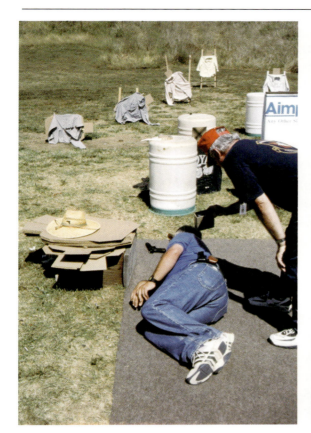

In the prone position, your arms should be extended and may or may not be supported. A prone draw is okay in training, as shown in bottom right photo, but in competition, you have the gun in hand in front of you <u>before</u> you go prone.

CHAPTER FOURTEEN
Practical Reloads

The International Practical Shooting Confederation competitions brought the semi-auto speed reload to its zenith. The speed reload is done with the slide forward and a round chambered; the mag is ejected and a fresh one inserted. Some competitors are able to do this in one second!

For IDPA competition, however, more practical reloads are mandated. The first is the Slide-lock Reload. Just as it sounds, the slide locks back on an empty magazine and the mag is ejected. A fresh mag is then seated and the slide is released, chambering a round. This is not too different from the IPSC Speed Reload. This is the reload that will most probably occur if the gun is used in self-defense, since you usually only reload when the "empty gun indicator" comes on - i.e., the slide locks back.

The other IDPA reloads are the Tactical Reload and Reload With Retention. The tactical reload, as taught by many world-class teachers, is predicated on the concept that when there is a lull in the fight you want to bring your firearm back up to full capacity.

The drill is simple. First you make sure you have a spare loaded magazine by locating it and bringing it to the gun. Next, since you normally have a limited amount of ammunition, you eject but hold onto the partially-depleted magazine and insert the new, fully-loaded magazine into the gun. The partially-empty mag is then stowed away in a pocket so that you still have the live rounds it contains. As to the correct way to hold the fresh magazine and capture the partially-empty one, there are two schools of thought.

Method A – I draw the fresh magazine from the carrier the same way for all reloads: My forefinger is extended on the face of the magazine, with my fingertip on the bullet nose of the top round and my thumb and the rest of my fingers holding the magazine. When I bring the fresh magazine to the gun, I eject the partially-filled magazine into my off-hand and capture it with my palm and the last two fingers.

Method B – Some schools teach that when you have the replacement magazine at the gun, you shift this magazine so that it is now protruding from between your middle and third fingers. Then you catch the partially-empty magazine with your palm, forefinger and middle finger and insert the fresh magazine.

Either method works with single-column magazines, depending on your manual dexterity, but everything falls apart when using double-column magazines. Method A may still work, but Method B probably does not, for the double-column magazine may be too fat to hold in your weaker fingers. Also, if a person has small hands, neither Method A nor Method B works. In this case, the "reload with retention" is the only option, since small hands are not physically capable of holding two double-column magazines.

To do a reload with retention, you first eject the partially-empty mag and pocket it, *then* find and insert the spare magazine. Actually, IDPA was hardly a few months old when an enterprising competitor used this method and noted that he had cut down on the motions necessary to get the gun loaded, thereby saving time and thus bettering his score. The problem is, your gun is down to one round for a longer period of time. Now, this is of no consequence in competition, but it could make all the difference in the real-world outcome!

Revolver shooters do similar reloads. If using a conventional speed loader (cartridges are held separately in the mechanism), empty and full rounds are ejected, the handful is stowed away and the cylinder recharged via the speedloader. A pragmatic sixgun user, wanting to maintain personal defense skills can, of course, simply remove the empty cases and replace them individually. If full- or half-moon clips are used, they are treated as are semi-auto magazines and must be retained if they contain any live ammunition.

All IDPA reloads are to be done from a position of advantage – behind cover or concealment if such is provided in the course of fire. A reload is considered completed when the fresh magazine, full/half-moon clip or individual cartridges have been inserted and, in the case of a revolver, the cylinder closed. To be in the "spirit" of IDPA, the partially-empty magazine should be put in a pocket or mag pouch prior to firing the next round. Since most tactical reloading is now done "off the clock," this should not be a problem. In the real world, of course, if a threat suddenly appeared you would fire whether or not the mag was properly put away.

CHAPTER FOURTEEN ~ *Practical Reloads*

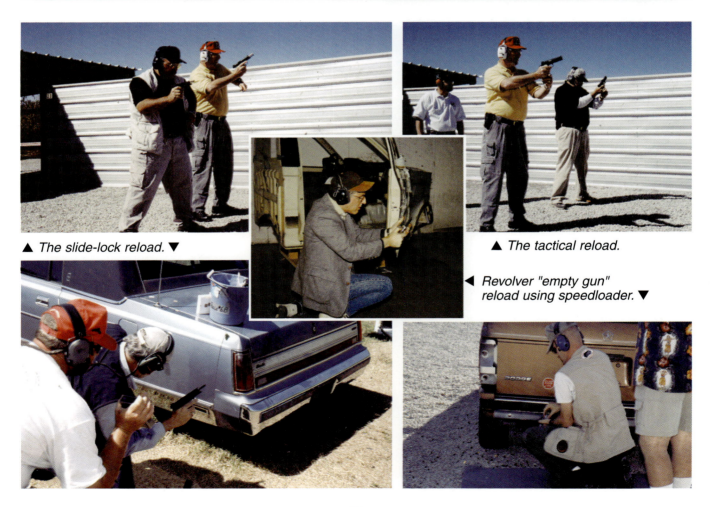

Two methods of making a tactical reload...

First Method: (1) Bring fresh magazine to the gun and retain it in a strong grip. (2/3) Remove and capture the partially-empty magazine while retaining a strong hold on the fresh magazine, then insert the fresh magazine into the gun.

Second method: (4) After grasping fresh magazine, shift it in your hand so that you can remove the partially-empty magazine with your thumb and forefinger. (5/6) Bring fresh magazine, captured between your fingers and palm, to the gun and insert.

▲ The slide-lock reload. ▼

▲ The tactical reload.

◄ Revolver "empty gun" reload using speedloader. ▼

CHAPTER FIFTEEN
Dim-Light Shooting

One of the more exciting course developments within IDPA is the resurgence of dim-light shooting stages that require either flashlights and night sights – or both. In the early years of the IPSC shoots, you were almost assured that sometime during the year you would get to shoot an entire match at night. For many of us in law enforcement, these night shoots were the only venue where we could practice our dim-light shooting techniques, because most police agencies had not yet moved in this direction. (Remember, this was at a time when a Mag-Lite was a new and treasured item!)

Night shoots went the way of the single-column 1911 in IPSC, but course designers in IDPA have brought them back – with the benefit now of a whole host of new flashlights and techniques to use them, as well as night sights on the guns.

Now a defense-oriented competitor can choose flashlights that range in size and intensity from those that fit in the palm of your hand to lights that can double as airplane beacons, along with a multiplicity of techniques for using them. Night sights also have become almost a mandatory item on a self-defense handgun. (And the single-column 1911 came back, too!)

How to use these devices has been the subject of many articles and books. A number of well-known writers and trainers have developed and named their individual techniques. One teacher in particular has contributed a great deal. Bill Rogers developed the technique of holding an end-cap-switch-activated light in between the fingers of your non-shooting hand, called, appropriately, the Rogers method. It's little known, but Bill was also the first to develop and teach the technique of holding a side-pressure-switch light in your non-gun hand and bringing both hands together in a modified isosceles shooting stance. This method was popularized by Ray Chapman in his courses at the Chapman Academy.

Massad Ayoob further modified this two-hand hold and created the Ayoob Technique. Michael Harries developed the concept of isometrically holding your two hands back-to-back with the end-cap light facing to the rear of your reversed non-shooting hand during firing.

I've found that extending the light forward from the center of my body during searching and then just bringing the gun's sights up into the light beam works well and quickly (the Rauch Method). Of course the old standby, the FBI method, still works well. Simply hold the light up and away from your body while shooting with one hand.

The night sights are there because of Murphy's Law, which says that if anything can go wrong it will. If the flashlight fails, you can still find and use your sights.

Dim-light shooting without using a flashlight can be done effectively.

CHAPTER FIFTEEN ~ *Dim-Light Shooting*

These photos illustrate various methods of using a flashlight.

Despite low ambient light, a flashlight is not needed in many situations.

CHAPTER SIXTEEN ~ *Designing IDPA Courses of Fire*

Courses of fire being shot at various IDPA matches.

CHAPTER SIXTEEN
Designing IDPA Courses of Fire

Coming up with at least one new, exciting and fun stage to run for every club match is an impossible task – if you wish to follow the intent of IDPA and its goals of using self-defense arms in a sporting atmosphere.

"Impossible" because self-defense, for the lawfully-armed non-sworn citizen, is almost always up-close-and-dirty and most often won't require you to fire a shot! If there is any shooting to be done, it's quick and dirty and the situation probably won't require you to run your gun dry. Of course, not too many shooters will pay to address a stage where they don't shoot. But I do think most shooters will understand and be able to relate to stages that "only" need four to six shots to complete.

If you want to get the round count up for the match, you can combine two or three potential scenarios and run them one after the other as a single stage. Or, better yet, start the competitors on Stage One and when they finish and reload, record the time, give them another start from where they're standing and go through the next part of the multiple stage. There's no down time. Just as they're done, give them 30 seconds to catch their breath, replace their two spare mags in their carriers and then move 'em out.

How do you find real-life problems that can be translated into a stage? Well, you've had at least a few experiences that could become match scenarios, I'm sure. Now, you're probably saying, "Yes, but they weren't shooting problems." Ah, but they might well have been had the circumstances been slightly different. All I'm asking you to do is reflect on your ordinary, everyday experiences.

Take a convenience store, for example. You're in line with five customers ahead of you. The door is to the front of the line. Three men, all wearing gang colors, enter the store and split up. One to your left and the other two go to your extreme right. No, this isn't a robbery, just three guys going for the coffee machine and the sandwich counter. But this *could have been* a life-threatening scenario if you were the store clerk and they split up to rob the store and the customers. (I grant you, there's a fine line between fantasizing that you're "Rambo" and looking at every encounter as a potential shooting problem, but you should be going through life watching for potential problems, anyway.)

In this scenario, you would not get involved if they were just robbing the store (not if you have a lick of sense!), but you would be in the soup if they took everyone's wallets and yours had your retired police ID in it!

In this instance, you have three shoot targets, all in the clear since all the no-shoots are in front of you. And while the bad guys are behind both hard and soft cover, you're also next to hard and soft cover (the grocery check-out counter and display). This could be three rounds to the 5-zone and then return with three head shots after you've taken your own, covered position.

OK, you don't have a clue. You live on a farm and never go to the nearby town, population 400, and there hasn't been a gun pointed in anger since the Civil War. In this instance, it's time to "borrow" ideas. Rick Miller, a Contributing Editor to *Combat Handguns* magazine, has been writing defensive shooting articles for over a decade and he conveniently supplies a sketch of shooting problems with most of his articles. Rick isn't just putting these in the magazine for laughs. I'm sure he'd appreciate someone taking these problems and using them. I've included some courses of fire based on my personal real-world experiences (with modifications). The scenarios as written were the beginning of the problems as I encountered them.

The following eight courses of fire, all based on actual incidents, could easily be used at your local club matches:

A BUY GONE BAD

Course Designer: Walt Rauch

You are seated in a booth with three men – one to your right and two across the table. The man to your right is the informant, the two men opposite are the "dealers." There is a crowded bar to your left, across the room. You are trying to make a "buy." The dealers want to rip you off. They have a back-up man at the bar.

Shooter, seated on a bench up against NT1, draws from beneath the table and engages T1 and T2 with one round each, then T3 at the bar with two rounds. Shooter then fires one head shot each at T1 and T2. Shooter remains seated during the encounter.

(**NOTE:** Shooter should perform a tactical or slide-lock reload at the end of the encounter.)

CHAPTER SIXTEEN ~ Designing IDPA Courses of Fire

A BUY GONE BAD

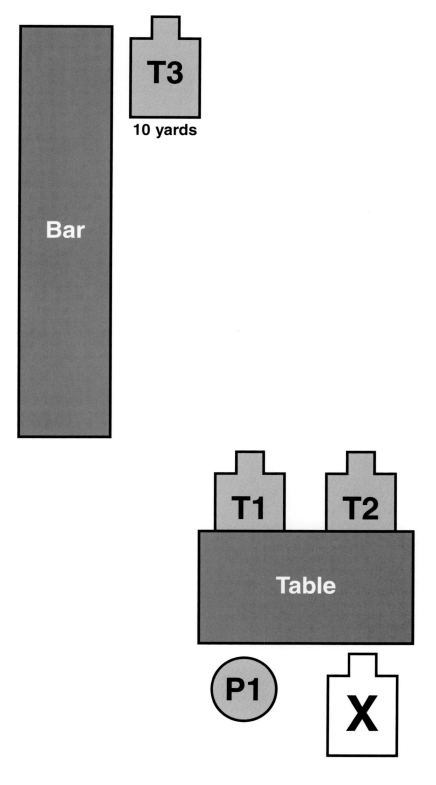

CHAPTER SIXTEEN ~ *Designing IDPA Courses of Fire*

THE "BOTTLE GANG"
Course Designer: Walt Rauch

As you park your car, you notice four men standing nearby. They are all drinking from bottles wrapped in brown paper bags.

As soon as you close and lock your car door and turn to the rear of the car, you are accosted by T1 and T2 at a distance of 10 feet. They ask for money. T3 has moved to the opposite side and rear of your car, while T4 is directly across from you on the opposite side of the car. (T3 and T4 are Pepper Poppers.)

Shooter engages T1 and T2 with one round each and backs up to the front of the car and engages T3 and T4. T3 and T4 can be engaged through windows, from beneath the car or from the front of the car.

(NOTE: Shooter should perform a tactical reload at the end of the encounter.)

CHAPTER SIXTEEN ~ Designing IDPA Courses of Fire

THE BOTTLE GANG

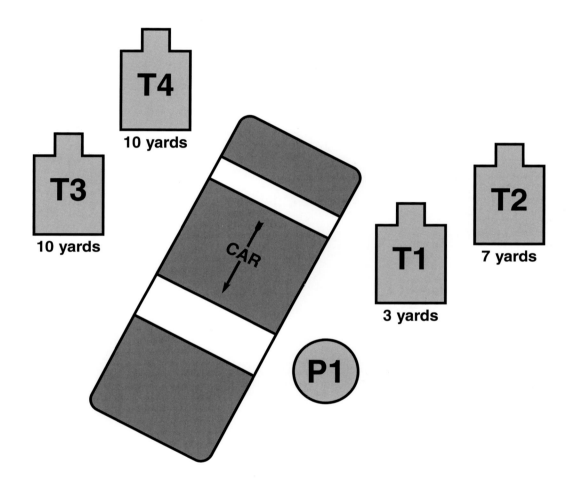

CHAPTER SIXTEEN ~ *Designing IDPA Courses of Fire*

HOT SURVEILLANCE ON CHESTER AVENUE

Course Designer: Walt Rauch

You are parked in a full-sized cargo van, sitting in the driver's seat. Three men approach the van. One positions himself directly in front of you (T1), while the second man (T2) goes to the passenger-side door. The third man (T3) is approaching the sliding cargo door on the side, which has a window in it. You are about to be carjacked!

Shooter, starting with gun in hand, engages T2 first, T3 second and T1 last. T2 and T3 require two head shots each, while T1 requires three rounds. Multiple rounds are needed to insure hits because shooter is firing through glass. Score all hits.

(NOTE: Shooter should perform a tactical reload at the end of the encounter.)

CHAPTER SIXTEEN ~ Designing IDPA Courses of Fire

HOT SURVEILLANCE ON CHESTER AVENUE

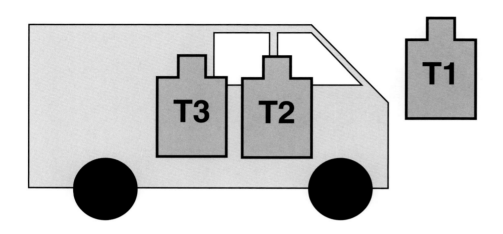

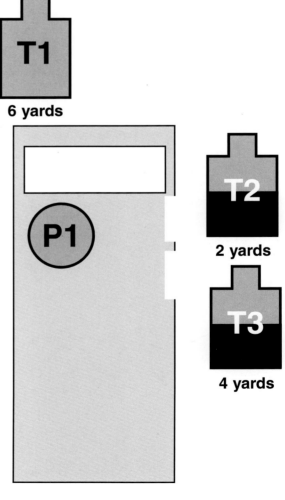

A LONG DRINK AT THE JOHNSTOWN BAR

Course Designer: Walt Rauch

You are seated at the bar on a high stool. Another patron, leaning on the bar to your right, takes exception to your looks, breaks a beer bottle off at the neck and announces his intention to carve up your face.

Shooter gets off the stool and backs up to the establishment's door, only to find it locked. Shooter must engage T1 with as many rounds as are in his gun because the threat is moving toward him very quickly.

(NOTE: Shooter should perform a tactical reload at the end of the encounter.)

CHAPTER SIXTEEN ~ Designing IDPA Courses of Fire

A LONG DRINK AT THE JOHNSTOWN BAR

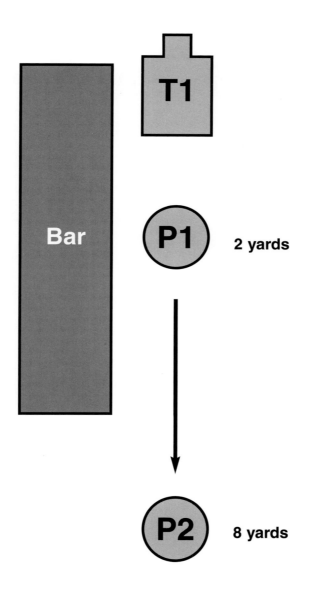

THE SAVINGS BOND WITNESS
Course Designer: Walt Rauch

You are conducting interviews in a residential neighborhood regarding stolen Savings Bonds and you find that one of your witnesses is not at home. A bystander volunteers to go get him from a house nearby.

As the volunteer and an unknown male you guess is your witness return to your location and approach you, the "witness" starts to draw a firearm from beneath his topcoat saying, "Draw, you scumsucker!" He is partially blocked by the volunteer.

Engage T1 but avoid shooting NT1. You cannot move to your left side because you're blocked by others on the sidewalk (NT2).

(NOTE: Shooter should perform a tactical reload at the end of the encounter.)

SAVINGS BOND WITNESS

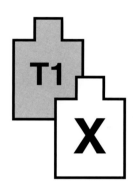

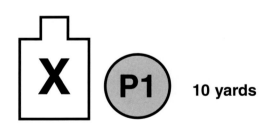

10 yards

CHAPTER SIXTEEN ~ *Designing IDPA Courses of Fire*

AN ORDINARY MUGGING

Course Designer: Walt Rauch

As you stand near your car waiting for your associate, four young men approach you and ask you for money. Since it is 2 AM and you and they are the only persons in the area, you surmise, correctly, that their intent is to rob you.

As they approach to within 10 feet of you in a tight cluster with no weapon visible, you step back and to either their left or right flank and engage them with your handgun.

Shooter starts at Position 1 facing four tightly-clustered targets, T1 through T4. Shooter engages all four targets with one round each as he moves rapidly to either the left or the right side of the four targets. Shooter should be at least to the outside edge of T1 or T2 before the first shot is fired.

(NOTE: Shooter should perform a tactical reload at the end of the encounter.)

CHAPTER SIXTEEN ~ *Designing IDPA Courses of Fire*

AN ORDINARY MUGGING

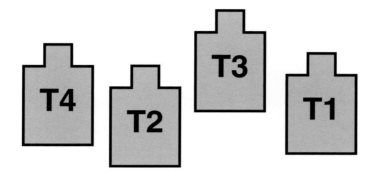

Targets are staggered three to five yards from P1 at arm's length from each other.

CHAPTER SIXTEEN ~ *Designing IDPA Courses of Fire*

AFTER THE BUY, STAY ALERT
Course Designer: Walt Rauch

You and your partner have successfully completed an undercover "buy" in a nightclub. You and he leave, but are greeted outside by four armed men who intend to rob you. You don't know if they are associated with the men you just left. There is no cover other than the club entrance from which you have just departed.

Shooter engages all targets with one round each, steps back into the doorway and, using the door jamb as cover, performs a tactical reload and re-engages all four targets.

(NOTE: Shooter should also perform a tactical reload at the end of the encounter.)

CHAPTER SIXTEEN ~ Designing IDPA Courses of Fire

AFTER THE BUY, STAY ALERT!

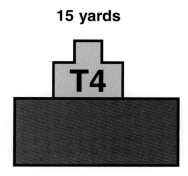

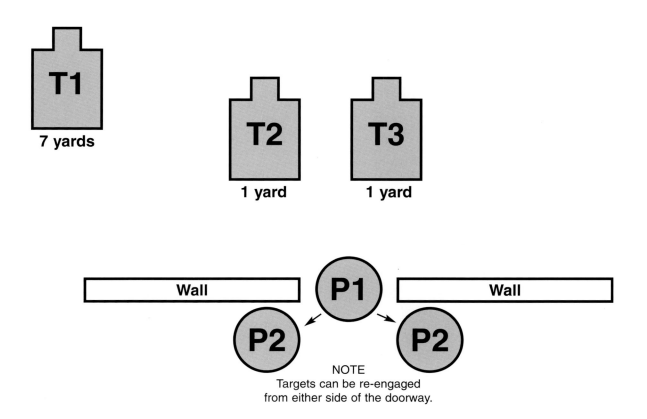

NOT ENOUGH GUN
Course Designer: Walt Rauch

You are "covering" four seated men (half-targets T1, T2, T3 and T4) in a living room while serving a warrant. One of them observes that you don't have "enough gun" to neutralize all four of them. En mass, they charge you from their chairs and couch. As you're taking them down, a female occupant of the residence (T5/Pepper Popper) tries to take you from the side.

Shooter starts with gun in hand at the low-ready position. He engages T1 through T4 with one round each, then engages T5, which is partially hidden by a wall, until it goes down. Given the 5-foot distance, T1 through T4 should be shot in two seconds or under.

(NOTE: Shooter should perform a tactical reload at the end of the encounter.)

CHAPTER SIXTEEN ~ Designing IDPA Courses of Fire

NOT ENOUGH GUN

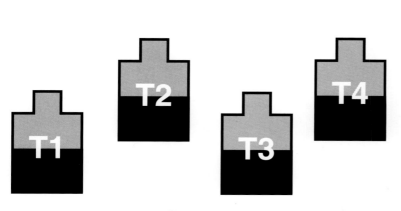
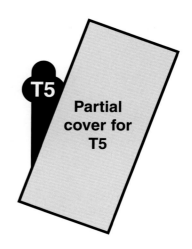

Stagger target distances from Position P1 plus or minus one yard.

 Approx. 4 yards

A Springfield Professional 1911

A Kimber Heritage 1911

CHAPTER SEVENTEEN
IDPA Classifier CL-0001

IDPA SAFETY OFFICER INSTRUCTIONS FOR CLASSIFICATION MATCH

Any Safety Officer preparing to administer the "Defensive Pistol" Qualification Match will want to review a number of factors prior to actual range firing.

> For any new shooters, each must have safe gun-handling techniques explained and demonstrated. New shooters should be asked to demonstrate basic speed draws, safe re-holstering, and reloading skills. Muzzle awareness should be carefully explained. Placement of the trigger finger in the trigger guard will only take place when the handgun is pointed downrange or at the target.
>
> S. O. should ask shooters if they have any questions concerning the range requirements and range orders.

It is wise to run each competitor through one stage at a time. At the end of each stage, score each competitor's targets and paste. If the contestant makes an error and has to repeat the stage, this way only one 30-round stage will have to be completed.

S.O. suggestions for Stage One

Remind the contestants that they cannot miss fast enough to win this event. Hits on the target are the goal. The goal is to get good hits on each string of fire.

For strings 1, 2, & 3 the shooter is recommended to position himself centered on target two. After the completion of string three, if the shooter has not reloaded his sidearm, the S.O. should tell the shooter to utilize a "tactical reload" prior to string four. This will be good practice for stage three.

In the "weak"-hand-only part of string five, a shooter should have the muzzle of the handgun positioned down at a 45-degree angle. Trigger finger must be outside the trigger guard, hammer may be cocked and safety off.

String seven is a strong-hand-only drill, and many shooters will be wise to start with their strong side toward the targets, allowing for a much more classic "dueling-type stance."

Stage Two

On string one, be sure and explain to the shooter that he must fire all six shots while moving forward. If he reaches the five-yard line before firing all six rounds, he will be penalized if he is firing any rounds while NOT moving. For best results the shooter should draw and begin firing as soon as possible. If the shooter takes a couple of steps before drawing and beginning to shoot, he will likely be at the five-yard line before he is finished shooting.

Warn the shooters to be careful when backing up and shooting in string two. Shooters should move smoothly and surely and this drill is designed to teach a person to place distance between themselves and the threat as quickly as possible while engaging the threat. All shots must be fired while moving.

In string three, instruct the shooter to load a magazine of 5 rounds in the handgun. There should already be a round in the chamber, thus he will have six rounds total in his sidearm. The goal here is to have the shooter shoot until his weapon will be empty. He must quickly reload and release the slide to charge the weapon and fire his remaining six rounds for the drill.

Stage Three

The key issue in the final stage is the "tactical reload." Shooters must be warned that the "tactical reload" requires the exchange of the partial magazine for a full one from behind cover. The partial magazine must be retained in a manner of practical carry. This means the partial magazine must be placed in a pocket, in the belt, or back in a magazine pouch. Lanyards, special baggy pockets, or placing the partial magazine in the mouth is not considered practical. If the partial magazine is dropped to the ground, the shooter may pick it up for retention without penalty. This is simply a standard reload for revolver shooters.

On string two the shooter is considered to be "LOADED" and may advance toward the barrel when the fresh magazine locks into place or revolver cylinder is closed. On string two and three, the shooter must use the barrel for cover and shoot from around the side; as such, shooter should be instructed to engage the far right target first if he is shooting from the right side of the barrel. Likewise if the shooter is engaging the targets from the left side, then he should engage the targets from left to right. This technique will teach the shooter to expose only a minimum of his body to the threat.

A wise S.O. will recommend that the shooter utilize a "tactical reload" between strings of fire and stages if possible. This will allow the shooter to become familiar with the technique of keeping his sidearm full and ready. Some range rules will require that the handgun be unloaded and maintained in a "cold" manner between stages. If possible, and range rules permit, the sidearm should be kept "hot" and ready for use.

If, during the actual firing of any stage, the shooter fails to follow instructions or makes an error, the shooter may be better off to repeat the stage to get a true picture of his skill. If penalties are used, the resulting score will not reflect the true skill level of the shooter and his "classification score" will be incorrect.

Many shooters may wish to shoot the IDPA "classification match" two or three times in practice before actual "shooting for score." The more familiar the shooter is with the stages, the less likely he is to make an error or have penalties.

CHAPTER SEVENTEEN ~ IDPA Classifier CL-0001

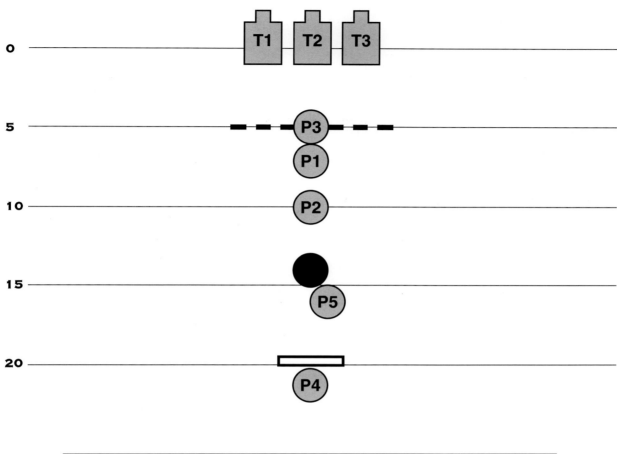

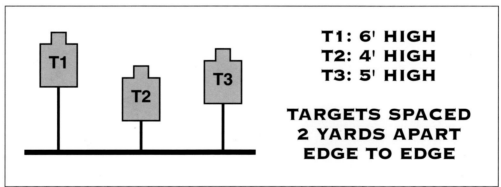

T1: 6' HIGH
T2: 4' HIGH
T3: 5' HIGH

TARGETS SPACED
2 YARDS APART
EDGE TO EDGE

**OFFICIAL
DEFENSIVE PISTOL CLASSIFIER MATCH
IDPA-CL-0001**

IDPA-CL-OOOI

CHAPTER SEVENTEEN ~ IDPA Classifier CL-0001

Defensive Pistol Classification Match

STAGE ONE - 7 Yards

String 1	Position #1	Draw and fire 2 shots to the body and 1 to head on T1.	3 shots
String 2	Position #1	Draw and fire 2 shots to the body and 1 to head on T2.	3 shots
String 3	Position #1	Draw and fire 2 shots to the body and 1 to head on T3.	3 shots
String 4	Position #1	Draw and fire 2 shots at each head Tl - T3.	6 shots
String 5	Position #1	Start gun in "WEAK" hand pointed down range at a 45° angle, safety may be off, but finger must be out of trigger guard, fire 1 shot at each Tl - T3. WEAK HAND ONLY.	3 shots
String 6	Position #1	Start back to targets, turn and fire 1 shot at each, Tl - T3, reload and fire 1 shot at each, Tl - T3.	6 shots
String 7	Position #1	Draw and fire 2 shots at each Tl - T3 "STRONG" hand only.	6 shots

STAGE TWO - 10 Yards

String 1	Position #2	Draw and advance toward targets, fire 2 shots at each Tl - T3 while moving forward (all shots must be fired while moving). There is a forward fault line at the 5yd line for this string.	6 shots
String 2	Position #3	Draw and retreat from targets, fire 2 shots at each Tl - T3 while retreating (all shots must be fired while moving).	6 shots
String 3	Position #2	(Load 6 rounds MAX. in pistol) Start back to targets, turn and fire 2 shots at each Tl - T3, reload from slidelock and fire 2 shots at each Tl - T3 .	12 shots
String 4	Position #2	Draw and fire 2 shots at each Tl - T3 "STRONG" hand only.	6 shots

STAGE THREE - 20 Yards *(Bianchi-style barricade and 55-gal. barrel required.)*

String 1	Position #4	Draw and fire 2 shots at each Tl - T3 from either side of the barricade, TACTICAL LOAD and fire 2 shots at each Tl - T3 from the opposite side of barricade.	12 shots
String 2	Position #4	Draw and fire 2 shots at each Tl - T3 from either side of the barricade, TACTICAL LOAD and advance to Position #5, fire 2 shots at each Tl - T3 from around either side of 55-gal. barrel.	12 shots
String 3	Position #5	Draw, kneel, and fire 2 shots at each Tl - T3 from around either side of 55-gal. barrel.	6 shots

Note: Start position for all strings EXCEPT Stage One / String 5 is hands naturally at your sides.

IDPA-CL-OOOI

Defensive Pistol Classification Match

STAGE ONE (30 Rounds Total, 10 Hits per Target Required)

BREAKDOWN OF CLASSIFICATION SCORES				
	CDP	ESP	SSP	SSR
Master	91.76	89.41	98.82	102.35
Expert	111.43	108.57	120.00	124.29
Sharpshooter	141.82	138.18	152.73	158.18
Marksman	195.00	190.00	210.00	217.50

Hits pet target

T1_____ T2_____ T3_____

String 1_____
String 2_____
String 3_____
String 4_____
String 5_____
String 6_____
String 7_____

_____Procedural x 3 sec _____
_____Points Down x .5 _____

Stage Total Time [____]

STAGE TWO (30 Rounds Total, 10 Hits per Target Required)

Hits pet target

T1_____ T2_____ T3_____

String 1_____
String 2_____
String 3_____
String 4_____

_____Procedural x 3 sec _____
_____Points Down x .5 _____

Stage Total Time [____]

STAGE THREE (30 Rounds Total, 10 Hits per Target Required)

Hits pet target

T1_____ T2_____ T3_____

String 1_____
String 2_____
String 3_____

_____Procedural x 3 sec _____
_____Points Down x .5 _____

Stage Total Time [____]

MATCH TOTAL [____]

Name_____
Address_____
City_____State____Zip_____

❏ CDP ❏ ESP ❏ SSP ❏ SSR
❏ MA   ❏ EX   ❏ SS   ❏ MM   Date_____

Ken Hackathorn, center, scoring targets at the IDPA Nationals.

CHAPTER EIGHTEEN ~ Scoring System

CHAPTER EIGHTEEN
Scoring System

The scoring system in IDPA has been much-simplified using a method developed by Larry Vickers and termed "Vickers Count" (VC). To arrive at the VC, take the total time to complete the string of fire plus the addition of five-tenths (.5) of a second per point dropped. Also add any other penalties incurred such as *Hits on Non-Threat Targets* - 5 seconds; *Failure to Neutralize* a target (any target with a point total of 4 points or less) - 5 seconds; *Procedural Error* - 3 seconds; and *Failure to Do Right* - 20 seconds to score. (*Failure to Do Right* is applied when a shooter doesn't comply with the spirit and intent of the scenarios.)

Standard Exercises are shot in a fixed time; penalties in the Standards are: *Procedural* -5 seconds; *Hits on Non-Threat Targets* – only one single 10-second penalty per target so shot, not a separate penalty for every bullet hole found on the target; and *Failure to do Right* - deduct 200 points from the total score!!

CONCLUSION

IDPA is a sport that offers an acceptable venue in which you can practice self-defense skills, but the founders of IDPA make no claim that mastery of every skill used in the sport will insure survival in a lethal confrontation. Understand that even if you become a Master shooter in all four divisions, winning every contest, you will still remain but a student of the art and science of self-defense. We all like to think the best of ourselves and our

A Garthwaite Custom Lightweight Commander.

abilities, so it is all too human to slip into denial about our own limitations, weaknesses and failings. Gunfighting is *not* a sport. There are few rules, but I've accumulated some that I follow regarding bad guys, conflicts and guns. I've also found many of these to be commonly-accepted observations by others who have lived with a gun. Murphy's Rules of Combat are also excellent. Here are some of mine:

Rauch's Rules
for the Real World:

1. All predators are always killers. When they attack, your options for self-defense are very limited.

2. The predator is smarter than you. Act and react accordingly.

3. Predators will use all the force necessary (and then some) to achieve their goals, without regard to consequences.

4. Predators evaluate their targets before attacking. If you are attacked, the predator has determined he will succeed without a heavy cost to himself.

5. If you are about to become a victim, you have already made serious mistakes.

6. Believe what you see; don't go into denial. Your attacker won't.

7. In a lethal confrontation, you will only have time to choose one course of action – and your life depends on making the right choice.

8. Predators rarely act alone, although the ones that do are the most dangerous. (If there's one, look for two; if there are two, look for three; etc.)

9. Fear is the predator's friend...and your enemy.

10. Talk and negotiation rarely work.

11. Predators do not have a conscience. Don't waste time and effort appealing to any sense of mercy or kindness.

12. Some people cannot be frightened or intimidated. Displaying a weapon may well not solve – and, in some cases, may exacerbate – the problem. Be prepared for this.

13. "Bullets don't work"...Gene Zink, a federal law enforcement trainer. No hand-held firearm fires a *guaranteed* "one-shot-stop" round. Anticipate needing follow-up shots.

14. "Stay plugged in. Stay in the fight"...Clint Smith, Director, Thunder Ranch.

15. Firearms don't work all the time and may well not work when you need them most.

16. Don't be overly concerned about caliber. No one wants to "leak" or have holes put in him.

17. Carry only the biggest-caliber gun you can control.

18. Carry a reload.

19. Carry a second gun.

20. Be able to get to both handguns with either hand.

21. Don't assume you can prevail in the conflict due to your superior tactics and training. The predator only has to be lucky once. Avoiding him is still the best defense.

22. The honest citizen pitted against a predator is an unequal contest. The predator is a professional. Most honest citizens are amateurs.

23. No competition or training, no matter how well learned or practiced, can equal hands-on experience.

24. Predators constantly validate their training with hands-on experience.

25. Getting hands-on experience can be fatal, but survivors learn their lessons well!

26. Expect to get shot!

27. When shot, don't expect to die.

28. If you are going to die, take him with you!